Streetwise
Prison Ministry

Streetwise
Prison Ministry

Rebecca Lewis

Archway Publishing books may be ordered through booksellers or by contacting:

Archway Publishing
1663 Liberty Drive
Bloomington, IN 47403
www.archwaypublishing.com
844-669-3957

ISBN: 978-1-6657-5624-2 (sc)
ISBN: 978-1-6657-5626-6 (hc)
ISBN: 978-1-6657-5625-9 (e)

Library of Congress Control Number: 2024902364

Print information available on the last page.

Archway Publishing rev. date: 04/03/2024

CONTENTS

Section One
The Realities of Jail and Prison Ministry

Section Two

Spiritual Traps in Jail and Prison Ministry

Section Three

Essays That Teach: Real People Applied Principles

SECTION ONE

The Realities of Jail and Prison Ministry

CHAPTER 1

Beginning Preparation for Jail and Prison Ministry

When I became a jail and prison chaplain over thirty-one years ago, I had a mission. It was simple: share the good news that is the gospel. It became important to be that presence of God to both inmates and officers in the very dark places that are jails and prisons. I understood the mission spiritually. But, in practice, I found it to be a different story. You can have all the parts to a puzzle, but putting them all together is a whole other ball game. It's a lifelong learning experience.

The title to this chapter, "Beginning Preparation," is an oxymoron. God begins to prepare you sometimes before you realize what the actual mission is. Beyond my onetime teenage desire to join the air force, dreaming of becoming an astronaut, I thought God was calling me to be a psychologist, a lawyer, or a police officer. I became familiar with those occupations. It was an adventure of exploration and listening and finding no satisfaction with those occupations.

But some adventures are pivotal. Part of my law enforcement exploration led me to doing an internship in a juvenile probation department in Jonesboro, Arkansas, under the supervision of Robert Nelms, the head juvenile probation officer. Two experiences from that internship were fundamental for my two years of chaplaincy internship at the Tarrant County Sheriff's Department in Fort Worth; my nine-year position as chaplain, then director of chaplaincy, at the Harris County Sheriff's Department in Houston; and, finally, my twenty years of chaplaincy with the Federal Bureau of Prisons. Mr. Nelms didn't give me much coaching. His idea of coaching was like throwing a kid into a lake to teach him to swim. You either swim or drown. So while watching from the bank, he threw a couple of cases at me with no instruction.

The first offender was a fourteen-year-old boy. I felt good about the counseling session. I was going to save this kid from himself, and I just knew my counseling would turn him from his criminal ways. After about twenty minutes, I was done. He hadn't said much, but I felt good about it. He seemed remorseful. When he left, I was giving my report to Mr. Nelms, thinking his beaming smile was an indication of praise to come for how well I had done. When I finished my report, he grinned and simply informed me that the seemingly remorseful young man had come for his probation check-in driving a stolen car.

The next case was an emotional teenage girl. She immediately turned on the tears. I responded by sitting next to her and putting my arm around her while she boo-hooed. She had really messed up. I could understand her tears. Nelms walked in on the touching scene and gave me another one of his knowing grins. The young girl immediately stopped her crying when he walked in and shifted her attention to the straight talk he gave her. I took a really good look at the girl while he was talking to her. For all the drama, she didn't have a single tear. That was my first introduction to crocodile tears.

From the first encounter, I learned a valuable lesson. My probationer's silence had not been agreement with my talk or even an indication he understood what I was saying. It had simply been silence. He'd probably tuned me out after hello and let his mind drift off to the next car he was going to steal. No breakthrough had occurred. All I'd done was make myself feel good.

The second encounter introduced me to emotional games people play. The crocodile tears of the girl had been a ploy to gain my sympathy to bait me for further manipulation. I was not helping her by being part of her cycle of emotion, which she'd probably used for years to gain sympathy but resulted in no decision to change her behavior. She was only upset she'd been caught.

I applied those lessons in how I approached dealing with inmates. One: stay issue oriented. Help them take responsibility and depend on God alone for validation. And, two: working with inmates is not a rescue operation. Stay out of your own emotions because sometimes the help we want to give is not helping. Plugging into the pain of the incarcerated and becoming part of the parade of people saying, "Poor baby," is allowing the inmates to add me to their long list of quick-fix, feel-good enablers.

Here's another layer to the bigger principle. Pack it in your tool belt. They don't need a quick fix spiritual lecture, and they don't need my sympathy. What I can give them is spiritual *truth* and the hope that they take responsibility for their own lives and turn to the God, who can give them life answers and healing. You and I have no power to make those decisions for them in their relationship with God. They have to make those decisions for themselves. They need that moment when they get honest with themselves. But we can offer them hope that day can come for them and trust the work of the Holy Spirit in their lives as we minister.

If you picked up this book thinking it was a simple how-to manual on prison ministry or a glowing narrative of victories that will inspire you, this is not it. Yes, I'm going to give you some basics, but I want to give you some information you probably didn't know you needed. Its information I've learned from the ground up as an insider working as a full-time jail and prison chaplain for thirty-one years in all kinds of correctional facilities, with all manner of staff and inmates, and with all types of law enforcement. Maybe this information can help equip you for that ministry right off the bat. I have to warn you that dispensing information like this is a bit like rounding up cats. There so many nuances of volunteering in jails and prisons that one subject will flush numerous rabbits. It's a struggle not to chase every rabbit. That's why you don't see many books like this. Those who work in jails and prisons as chaplains or religious volunteers could fill volumes.

Be forewarned. This is not a religious pep talk. I'm not into fluffy religiosity. Some of the information may shake up your ideology and maybe your theology. But don't be concerned. Our belief in God's plan for us encompasses the big picture that started well before the literal birth of Christ. My faith isn't dependent on the baby in the manger but the fulfillment of the King on the throne. And a king tells it like it is and wants people to be strong and wise in his service. I intend to bring you the map of ministry in jails and prisons so you can be wise in how you share the gospel in these dark places. My purpose is to equip the reader with knowledge and reality regarding the nature of ministry behind bars and perhaps create some streetwise people of faith who present the gospel to the incarcerated effectively.

CHAPTER 2

The Difference between Jail and Prison Ministry

If you're new to jail or prison ministry, let's make sure you know the difference between the two. This is generic information for the most part.

Jail populations and policies are a bit of a mishmash, so what might be true for one jail may not be true for another. Take pieces of this information and build your own application to the jail in which you are serving. It can be confusing.

The larger percentage of people in jails are not sentenced or not long term. If they don't bond out, they may sit in jail awaiting trial. Yes, people do time in jail, and some who are sentenced on the county or city level can do sentences in jail. Others, having been sentenced to prison, may have to wait a while to be transferred. But jails are fundamentally temporary and transitory.

I've always called ministry in jails popcorn ministry because it's like a kernel of popcorn. You never know when the population is going to change. Jails are pretty fluid. Inmates will go to court, get sentenced, be transferred to a prison, be moved to another floor, or be released. This makes jail ministry essentially a spiritual triage. You are interacting with people who are in stressful, unsettled circumstances. You may only get one shot at that individual. That should cause you to tailor your approach to religious topics and counseling opportunities to that reality when ministering in jails.

An inmate once told me how he saw his jail situation. He said he may run up on a curb and lose a hubcap, but the jolt makes him get back on the road. Some inmates go in and out of jail like going up on a curb. Sometimes, it takes several trips to jail before they wake up. A religious volunteer in that crisis moment has great influence on redirecting that person before their jail time turns into a long stretch in prison because of uncorrected behavior.

Jail ministry is the ultimate meeting of a person where they are in their life, both figuratively and literally. They've run up on that curb, and they may be ready to listen and correct what's going on in their life. That calls for direct talk to them and simple gospel concepts. You never know how profound that short interaction may be. You may be the whisper of God in the consequences of them experiencing the behavioral wreck that landed them in jail. But then, like a wisp of smoke, you may never see that person again. You have to learn the art of listening and discernment and the ability to let go of the emotional place they are in so you can effectively hear what they really need in the moment. Remember Jesus and the woman at the well, and you will get the idea. Jesus just cut to the chase.

In contrast, prison is long term. The first few weeks an inmate enters a prison, they are trying to adjust mentally and physically to a place that will be their so-called home for several years. Chapel attendance may be regular, but after they settle in and get their emotional footing, chapel attendance slacks off as they settle in to various other routines that emotionally help them survive. Get ready for that, and don't take it personally. God is working in their lives in ways you don't know, and the bottom line is they have to want to make changes.

If you come in on a regular basis, there will develop a core group of inmates that will come to your studies, and it will allow you to do deeper studies and counseling over a period. You become important to their spiritual growth every time you come in. You bring a little touch of normalcy in their abnormal world.

It's not an easy ministry. Be aware: the long-term nature of prisons does make your mission more complex. Prisons are a mirror of society complete with issues of race, politics, aberrant behaviors, territory issues, family dynamics, sexual deviations, workplace dynamics, and a multitude of religious issues.

Depending on the custody level of the prison, the inmate has the ability to move around a bit more, goes to recreation, has a work assignment, eats in a large dining area, and has access to education and chapel areas. Hourly timed movement, often just ten minutes that allows the inmate to move from one place to another, is a norm, and numerous official head counts take place. Those factors provide the possibility of the interruption of an inmate's regular attendance in chapel, even with the best intentions.

Additionally, those emotional issues they had stuffed down to deal with later while attempting to evade the consequences of their actions during their season of jail and court now present themselves front and center in odd ways. Some may enter a grieving process because of separation from family or loss of power and status on the street. Many are angry or fearful or continue to act out, making no changes in spite of where their previous actions have landed them.

Those emotional tensions can bleed out in their prison situation, so they often exaggerate defensively their religious beliefs just for some solid ground to stand on. This means you should expect some inmates to passionately try to engage you in religious debate. Since the chapel is a place where many religions practice their faith, there's also a chance for a type of religious tension to develop between groups and even denominational competition, so be ready to encounter that.

A large percentage of those in prison will seek the chapel religious programming, at least initially, to give themselves some hope and solace while they settle in and figure out where to go from there. That's where availability of volunteers and chaplains from all faiths is beneficial. Inmates will still have to decide if they want to invest in change while incarcerated. But the long-term programming with consistent volunteers provides them with that opportunity to start while they are locked up, and it may translate to a lasting change when they are released.

CHAPTER 3

Basics before Visiting

Now that the elementary differences of jail and prison have been touched on, let's start with how to begin coming into those places. From making a visit to a church member to being interested in doing regular volunteering, there are some basics that will help you. Working within any government entity can get frustrating, so here are some hints.

If you are internet savvy, go online and look up the institution. Most jails and prisons have websites. You click on the city or county, and it will pull up the name of the chief of police, sheriff, jail administrator, number of inmate beds, and even general inmate identity location and provide you with basic phone numbers.

State and federal prisons also have websites with a state and national inmate database. But, often, there are no direct numbers to chaplains. You have to go through the main number and be directed to those numbers and people. That can get frustrating if their phone systems aren't working right. But on the websites, there are usually email addresses for the people who deal with the public. If you are having trouble getting through the public line, they need to know that. Any savvy public official does not want the ire of the public, so they will respond and get your request to the person you have tried to call. But use that email system to let them know their public phone system is not working.

That last comment flushed an information rabbit. Be aware if you are calling about a specific inmate to visit; there are inmates whose identity and location are protected, and you may not get the information even if you do get through. You will be referred elsewhere.

That hitch aside, you can't beat making that call and talking to an actual human who can tell you how all that information is applied. In truth, if you just walk in off the street to the lobby, you are going to be viewed as a bit strange and get off to a rough start. Having a bit of information prior to showing up will save you time, embarrassment, and, for sure, aggravation.

Each facility will have visiting procedures that are similar but will be different enough to keep you off balance. One facility may allow you just to show up and show a pastoral credential and some form of identification, and in you go. This is sometimes true for very small jails. Others require prior association with the inmate and your name be listed by the inmate as minister of record on a preapproved visiting list. This is especially true with inmates who are in the media spotlight. You can imagine there are well-meaning clergy that focus on that type of inmate eager to get their souls saved. But, sadly, there are also the inevitable charlatans that are no more than spiritual ambulance chasers who insert themselves into that spotlight as their deliverer.

Jails and prisons usually have a titled shift supervisor. Titles may include information officer, operations lieutenant, shift commander, or desk sergeant. Sometimes, there's a daytime front desk officer that deals with incoming calls and the public who enter the front lobby.

Depending on time of day, if you do get through, like shift changes or evening hours, your call may go right to the heart of the control center, which is the lifeline of the facility. These officers have to watch monitors full of inmate and staff movement, call move times in the institution, hand out and receive radios and keys for staff, and respond to emergency issues on the compound or unit, such as initiate staff response to a fight, or medical emergencies, and the like. Asking for the shift supervisor will get you to a person, which will probably be more specific in their responses because they are not in the actual hands-on hub at the time. It may also keep you from getting the brush off from the person answering the phone who may be involved in institutional multitasking.

By the way, jails and prisons have at least three shift changes. Calling at shift change is not a good idea. It would be good to find out when those shift changes are if you want at least a type of quality information getting conversation with whoever answers the phone.

The larger prisons and jails will have a full-time chaplain. I'd recommend the first question you ask is if they have that full-time chaplain on duty and ask to speak to them because you know then you'll get the attention from someone who understands where you are coming from. But if there is no chaplain, ask your questions of the person who answers the phone and see where that takes you. Most of the time, they will give you information regarding types of visitation including religious programming if they aren't too busy.

Let me point out also that just because you are calling and know who to ask for, you cannot know what has gone down such as a fight in the prison or jail prior to your call. So, if you don't make contact with the right person willing to answer your questions, don't get all upset, just call back later. But do call back. The squeaky wheel gets the oil eventually. Be patient.

The following questions will help those just making a prison or jail visit. These questions are relatively just for those wanting to know how to start visiting. I'll get more in depth later for volunteers and clergy coming to do a worship or study service of some kind. Remember, there are no stupid questions. And knowing what to ask actually starts to build up your credibility to the staff. They will recognize that you aren't just some loony coming off the street. I say that because correctional staff will be suspicious because of the nature of their job.

Here are a few questions you may want to ask.

- What are the regular visiting days and hours? Jails may have more flexible visiting schedules, but prisons most often will have only two or three days set aside for visitation.
- How far in advance of the visit should I be there? There are entry procedures, which include logging in, getting ID badges, going through metal detectors and sometimes pat downs, all of which will add to your entry time.
- Can I give the inmate anything? Contraband items enter jails and prisons often. This perpetuates rules not allowing anything to be directly given to the inmate. Some smaller places will allow you to leave literature, but many will require you mail it in, and there are even

rules regarding what and how something can be mailed in. For instance, in the federal system, a preapproved form has to be sent to the vendor to be enclosed with the article to be mailed. The literature has to be mailed directly from the bookstore to prevent a third person, such as family, from having contact with the item and potentially inserting contraband. It can be complicated, but it cuts down on contraband. Even then, contraband still makes it in. Inmates are clever, and so are their families and friends.

If you are actually coming in to do a religious study of some kind, and your church wants to supply the books or bibles, large amounts are more practical being mailed in to the chaplain. That way, security scanning can be done and take up less time for staff when doing entry scanning. Small amounts of literature that you can hold in your hand may be allowed in along with your own personal Bible, but these items will have to be preapproved and go through the front lobby scanner or hand searched. Even your Bible may be searched. Don't be so naïve as to think no one has ever tried to get contraband in stuck between the pages of a Bible. It's not about you or questioning your integrity as a person of faith. It's about maintaining the integrity of the security within the institution. It doesn't matter if you've been in the same facility fifty times and they know you. Don't give the entry officer problems. Empty your pockets, open your Bible for searches, and don't take it personally. They are just doing their jobs. It's trust but verify.

- I am a member of the clergy. What kind of credential do I need? A clergy visit is only for the ordained of a faith. Most clergy will have an official card from the denomination. If not, then a credential associating you with the church works most of the time. If the person is delegated minister for prison ministry from the church, but not clergy, most places will require a letter of validation on letter head from the pastor of the church stating you are visiting on behalf of the church.

  Don't be insulted by being asked for your credentials. You must realize requiring identification is vital to security. It generally has nothing to do with questioning your honesty. Family members and ambulance chasers often want the ability to have the visiting privileges afforded clergy and lawyers. Identification validates you and assures the integrity as well as the security of the visit.

  If you are relative of the person incarcerated and also a clergy, that's a gray area. You come under suspicion immediately as one who is trying to use clergy privilege just to skip regular family visitation and potentially have physical contact. Don't use your clergy status to visit with a family member. It runs down on credibility for other clergy. Get another clergy to do that spiritual visit with family. Common sense will tell you an impartial person would be more able to get through to your relative. Family is too invested. Remember: my remarks here are just regarding clergy who have a family member incarcerated seeking to use their clergy title to bypass

> regular visitation. You can always visit during family visitation clergy or not.
>
> In some places, inmates must have filled out a list of persons they authorize to visit. Their chosen clergy should be on that list. It's called clergy of record. Clergy visits for the most part are by request of an inmate rather than clergy initiated. Clergy the inmate does not know won't be allowed to visit unless approved by the inmate.

These rules are for a reason. There is always a lot of interest from community clergy following a high-profile case. For instance, when Tim McVey, the Oklahoma City bomber, was temporarily housed at the federal prison in El Reno, Oklahoma, many people called interested in his spiritual welfare. None would be permitted to visit with him since there were no former ties prior to his offense. He turned down numerous requests from clergy who wanted to visit with him. He wanted nothing to do with God or the many donated bibles that total strangers sent in to him to the chapel. It was all his decision. The point is, if the inmate doesn't have you on his clergy of choice list, you won't be allowed to visit even during regular visitation.

Some places have *inmate-visiting points,* which cut off family visits when they are used up. Visitation time limits may also exist. This is because of crowding in visitation rooms. Some clergy I have known don't mind coming on regular family visitation days if it doesn't take away from the inmate's ability to visit with their family during the month. Clergy visits shouldn't be deducted from those points, so make sure you tell the duty staff it's a clergy visit if you choose to visit during family visitation time.

You can see there are many variables particular to clergy. So, as clergy, here is another question to ask: I want a private clergy visit with this inmate. Where will my visit take place? Family and friends, of course, will visit in areas common to a particular jail. Some are through a glass; other places have an open visitation room, and you visit with others at tables or chairs. An officer and/or cameras are always monitoring.

Clergy most often can have contact visits and are not required to visit during regular family visitation time. Some places have special visiting areas set aside for clergy and lawyers, but in other places, it will not be a contact visit. At times, you will really have to respectfully insist on the clergy penitent privilege if you want some level of privacy.

I recommend already knowing what your state or federal laws are on the subject and then how the particular institution has applied that law. It can prevent on-site friction with staff. Stay respectful, and simply go up the chain of command if you aren't satisfied with the policy, but not in the moment. Jails and prisons are places of routine operation and don't take well to surprise requests. Again, do your homework for the particular facility and how they apply clergy request, then go from there if you don't think policy or the law is being followed.

Coming in for a private clergy visit shouldn't be taken for granted. Please respect the bigger picture. Clergy and attorney visits require more attention and thus may be a bit irritating to staff that are already overworked and understaffed. It's nothing personal against clergy if staff seems a bit testy when dealing with you. Both clergy and attorney visits require special handling, and extra staff may have to be utilized. Remember: the institution doesn't just stop when you arrive. Assigning a staff member to monitor a private meeting is invasive to the orderly running of the place. You are the public, and they will follow policy in place, but you may get some resistance. A monitored clergy or lawyer visit often takes more than an hour of a staff member's time depending on the logistics of such a visit.

You might have caught the word *monitored*. There are really no visits where no scrutiny exists. While staff may not be in the room with you listening, you still may have to be visible to them. I could give many examples of clergy and lawyers passing contraband to an inmate. That's why the suspicion. There's also a safety issue. Clergy and attorneys have been attacked by inmates who take out their anger on the very people who would help them. It's like a wounded dog. A person in pain is unpredictable, and when things don't go their way, they bite. So, don't get upset if a staff is in the area or you are on camera. You should have a reasonable expectation of clergy penitent privacy, but that may not include absence of monitoring.

CHAPTER 4

The Value of Religious Volunteers

Volunteers become part of the complex dynamic of the institution's management of religious practice. The ability to actually share the gospel where people can have their own encounter with God in a prison setting depends a lot on functioning wisely within the walls of that setting. Jail and prison ministry is truly going into the hard-core mission field where thousands are sinking fast from personal destruction. Many people who volunteer to venture into the belly of the beast of jails and prisons are given instructional dos and don'ts regarding this mission. However, once you hear the loud clank of the steel doors closing behind you, the whole environment can be overwhelming. The realization hits you that the usual barebones information you are given in orientation was just not enough to prepare you. You can do more harm than good when you don't invest personal time in learning as much as you can about any mission God has for you, much less the dark places that are our jails and prisons. It's a bigger picture than just doing a church service, small group Bible study, or one on one.

Jail and prison volunteers are the often unappreciated saints of God. These people go into our jails and prisons weekly throughout our country offering God's unearned love to thousands of the castoffs of society. What would possess these so-called bleeding hearts to be driven to bring grace to even some of the most rebellious and sometimes evil in our society? How dare they bring a message of peace and spiritual freedom and even forgiveness to murderers, thieves, embezzlers, child abusers, drug dealers, and rapists. Many in society don't understand and even resent these attempts to bring redemption to these "dregs of society," some deeming them unfit even to breathe free air ever again. But if we are ever going to deal effectively with recidivism, you can't ignore the spiritual hole in a person. The offer of redemption and forgiveness doesn't translate to dismissal of consequences for actions. It just brings the opportunity for the inmate to regroup spiritually, which in turn creates a better environment in the units and in interaction with not only staff who work in these places 24/7 but also their families who are affected by their incarceration. Relationship with the Lord leads to the inmate accepting personal responsibility for their actions. That relationship evolves into a change of behavior and perhaps a life well lived after release or a life well lived throughout incarceration.

Volunteers, I think you're crazy for even doing this ministry. I often have jokingly said this to some of the most precious people in God's kingdom. Most volunteers are not hand holders. They are not ministering in jails and prisons because they have nothing else to do. They come from all levels of education and professions. They are dedicated and called to this ministry. Weekly, they come into a dark place full of broken people to share the light of the gospel and an encouraging word to those people who have found themselves on the dung heap of society and doing time. And yet from their pits of desolation, these inmates see these righteous people enter their domain with the gospel offering them hope. I've known chronic lawbreakers who finally got their feet on the ground and break that cycle of behavior because their newfound relationship with Christ gave them the courage to overcome their addictions in whatever forms those addictions translate. Volunteers played a big part of that.

The possibility of lower recidivism exists for inmates who deal with their spiritual life while locked up. I'll tell you straight up, without that foundation spiritually, all the secular education programs are like building a house on sand. Religious volunteers give counsel, worship services, and small group bible studies. They include those groups who bring structured reentry programs that deal with the whole person spiritually, mentally, and physically and will impact positively jails and prisons and ultimately society.

Most inmates have some kind of release date. But what kind of hope can be offered to a man who has wasted his life in crime, alienated his family, and will die in prison? The impact of volunteers on jail and society often extends beyond just the inmate.

There was a precious older couple that rarely missed a week in coming to minster at the federal medical center where I was a chaplain. This place is where the chronically ill doing federal prison time are sent to either heal or finish out their life. In the course of this man's last days, his teenage daughter, who had never met her father, had searched him out only to find him dying in prison. They had corresponded briefly, and she wanted to meet him. The dying inmate shared with the volunteer couple regarding his daughter and his missed years of her life. I don't think there was actually a time where she was able as a teenager to travel from out of state to meet her father face-to-face. But when he died, she was adamant on attending his funeral.

The prison contracts with a free world funeral service and bury inmates who have no one left who cares to receive their body. They are buried in a type of pauper's section of a cemetery. That was the case with this inmate. Ordinarily, it's a graveside funeral with the chaplain and the funeral service representative. And that's only for the casket to be opened and the chaplain to identify that the body of the inmate is actually being buried, not some weird escape attempt, and to say a few words over the body.

In this case, exceptions were made. These volunteers were allowed to pick up the daughter at the airport and bring her to the graveside that day. Their ministry to the dad triggered a ministry far more reaching in the life of his daughter—though she would not have the relationship with her dad she'd always wanted—whose first and last moments with her father would be healing in her life and full of the grace of God ushered in by this volunteer couple whose ministry to prisoners brought reconciliation to this young woman and her father. Those last moments by the grave completed her journey and sent her on another in life that would be full of hope because of the willingness of this volunteer couple to extend their love to this young woman, giving her a last gift of her father. At the end of a vanquished life of failures, the inmate had repented of his wasted life and introduced his daughter to the hope he had found in Christ through last letters.

This couple would go on to help the young woman heal and grow in her own relationship with the Lord. That sunny day by the grave completed a season of life for the dead inmate and his daughter. Both started new lives, one by death, entering into eternity with Christ, and the other by the healing touch of God on a young girl's life who found hope in her future because of a dedicated prison ministry volunteer couple.

Why a person is locked up doesn't matter to religious volunteers. Their mission is to introduce them to the Lord. Keep your skepticism regarding motives of people who minister in jails and prisons if you wish, but leave room for that one person that gets their life together because a religious volunteer gave them a boost of hope to try again. Yes, I think people like that are crazy for coming in to minister in prisons. But if that's crazy, I'll take it anytime.

CHAPTER 5

The Role of Chaplains

I'd wager most of you have a limited view of the role of the chaplain in corrections. Chaplains are not just glorified program directors in the institution. These corrections chaplains multitask, and their tentacles of support go into all parts of the institution. They are invaluable to both inmate and staff. Most have college degrees, seminary degrees, and many have some form of correctional and law enforcement or military background. There are even adjunct chaplains that are very professional in their own right who give their time voluntarily, are trusted by sheriffs, and are given some measure of authority and access to the jail.

Chaplains aren't watchdogs for the administration. They work within the system while not embracing the politics of that system. Neither are they inmate advocates taking on an inmate's complaints from those experiencing discipline born of their own behavior. But they will engage issues of right and wrong and speak truth to power on behalf of inmate and staff. They can be that buffer in a system whose mission deals daily with the castoffs of society. Your facility is fortunate if they have a chaplain coordinating inmate religious programming and being available to inmate and staff.

While not being watchdogs inside the system, a chaplain's mere presence can calm a situation. I recall a time when I was working a large-capacity jail that had eleven stories. I was making rounds on a unit floor and walked around a corner of a long hallway. Two officers had hands on an inmate who was resisting them. The volatility of the altercation resulted in the inmate being appropriately, albeit roughly, placed face-first against the wall. Simultaneously, the officers and inmate turned to look at me and froze. The next moment was like a director yelling, "Cut!" It was as though someone turned off the tension. No more resistance came from the inmate, and the officers were able to moderate their level of response to the inmate and got him under control. I had said and done nothing. All I did was stand out of the way while the officers moved him on down the hallway. Chaplains are that emotional buffer and neutral zone for both inmate and staff. The clergy factor brings some presence of light and calm to a place that is always a spark away from conflict.

When it comes to dealing with inmate religious issues, more and more state, county, and city administrators of jails and prisons recognize the value of having that buffer between the secular and the spiritual. Administrators and correctional staff have other things to do other than deal with religion and volunteers. When they find that person they can trust with the responsibility, they couldn't be more happy than to let them deal with the religious volunteers and inmates and, yes, even staff with counseling support. Having a chaplain on staff is a plus for public relations too as the public for the most part sees chaplains as a neutral entity in the institution. It's a tenuous walk on a tightrope for the chaplain dealing with the public, inmates, inmate families, staff, and their families. So when you encounter a chaplain, know the prison administration or sheriff has entrusted them with a very important and complex role.

The level of authority given to a chaplain varies. On the jail level, it's more arbitrary. It depends on the sheriff and his trust in the person he's chosen to run the volunteer programs. Sometimes, a sheriff contracts with a person or agency to supply chaplains, and they are treated just like agency staff complete with access to all parts of the jail and provided an office inside the jail. At other times, a sheriff selects a volunteer that has shown trustworthiness and some measure of common sense, and they are given a level of clearance by the sheriff to function inside the jail. In state and federal systems, with some exceptions, chaplains are part of the paid staff, and their duties are written in job descriptions. But the fact a jail or prison has a chaplain with given authority is what you need to respect.

As their duties relate to religious volunteers, a chaplain is overseer, initiates the background check—meaning, depending on the institution, they will do it themselves or get it to the volunteer coordinator who does the security training—helps provide training to religious volunteers relevant to institutional policies regarding security, and sets schedules and monitoring of volunteers and necessary floor or room assignments for programs. They also provide staff with education and updates as to how religious volunteers function inside the institution and provide up-to-date information on religious issues and laws and how those things are implemented in jails and prisons. That information keeps staff out of the hot seat from litigation-obsessed inmates who push back at the system and file lawsuits at the drop of the hat for perceived violations of religious rights. A chaplain who knows their stuff is invaluable to jail and prison administrators.

CHAPTER 6

Chaplains and Volunteer Friction

Volunteers, chaplains are there to make coming into an institution to minister smoother. It's a complex role, so listen up. Please don't pick fights with the chaplain. And unless something is especially egregious, don't go over their heads to the administration. Did I get your attention? I hope so. What kind of conflict can possibly affect chaplain and volunteer interaction? It usually comes from a volunteer who lacks understanding of how much like a labyrinth the practice of religion is in prisons and jails. They then plug into a complaint from an inmate associated with their faith group.

Chaplains have to make all kinds of unpopular decisions regarding the practice of religion, and sometimes that may curtail full implementation of certain practices that may clash with security or another religion. Inmates may see that as a violation of their rights and may seek to draw volunteers into the internal institutional decision-making process. Rest assured, the chaplain has researched and considered every aspect of an inmate's request for some kind of religious accommodation to find the least restrictive possibility for religious expression while they are doing time.

Where does that tension come from? I'll point out a few possible things. A little known variable chaplains deal with are volunteers who think that if the chaplain isn't of their own faith, they are innately prejudiced against them coming in to minister or stonewall them after they do get access. As a residual of that belief, some think, if they allow themselves to be under the authority of a chaplain not of their denomination, they are condoning the chaplain's beliefs, and that sets them up to get testy with the chaplain in the name of holding the fort for their denominational creed. Volunteers should remember it's not about agreeing with the beliefs of that chaplain. It's about the respect for the *role* they have been given. Facilitating groups not of their faith is part of their job.

A primary complaint by those suspicious of the motives of a chaplain is the perception they have treated them unfairly regarding program access. I'm not saying those chaplains don't exist, but they are not the standard. Those chaplains have lost their way and have not been able to find that balance between working for a secular entity and the practice of their own faith. Religious expression and practice is an individual choice. The impression that a chaplain is inhibiting their perception of how to practice their own faith can start the dominoes falling in the chapel. Those types of complaints are quickly investigated.

The reality is the majority of chaplains are professionally able to facilitate all faiths equitably. That means they concentrate on what that particular religion mandates and are necessary to adequately practice of their faith in the jail or prison setting. Chaplains will respond to any religious need of inmates curtailing only those areas of religious practice that will impact security or the smooth running of the institution.

Be aware. Chaplains give counsel to anyone who comes to them regardless of religious preference, even perhaps inmates from your denomination. How Jesus interacted with people was my model for being a chaplain in jails and prisons. Jesus interacted with people of all faiths without compromising what he was trying to teach. Because of that, inmates of all faiths, including those of non-Christian religions, sought me out for counsel. Inmates and staff were aware of my particular denominational choice. That never put off someone from seeking me out if they had a problem. Some just came to chat, others to discuss and maybe have friendly debate on religious differences, while others came with ongoing struggles they couldn't overcome, including institutional red tape issues they needed corrected. Sometimes, a chaplain can look into a matter that rightfully needs to be addressed by staff, such as inmate-to-inmate abuse or a medical issue that has fallen through the cracks.

Those types of encounters are opportunities for counsel. Chaplains don't have to neuter themselves from their own religious viewpoint to be fair and balanced in how they interact with inmate or volunteer. A chaplain models understanding grace and tough love. The majority of chaplains do not take advantage of the struggles of a person to browbeat them or oppose a brand of religious expression in the name of Christ. I did look at each encounter as an opportunity to listen and interact with that person in a manner that would impact their ability to have an encounter with Christ. But nothing was forced or coerced, and neither was the message inhibited. It's kind of like what Jesus did with Zacchaeus, the woman at the well, or even Pilate. He just spoke truth.

My standard lead line when someone came to me with an issue was to ask what faith they were and if they were practicing their faith. I would remind them that my counsel would be coming from my foundations of faith, and if we continued in the counseling, I would not shy from that. If they still wanted to talk, I'd pray for wisdom in how I dealt with that particular person.

Sometimes, you have to cut though the weeds to get to the real issue when inmates complain to you as a volunteer. I'd encourage you not to place the chaplain you are working with at your particular facility in an adversarial role with you simply because they are of a different faith. Please put it in perspective. Jails and prisons are public entities, and chaplains have to find balance in response to inmate religious needs within that framework. An appointed or paid chaplain must *facilitate* all faiths. Make the distinction that, while the chaplain is *facilitating* various religions, even non-Christian ones, it does not mean that chaplain is *promoting* them. The role of the chaplain regarding volunteers not of their own faith simply is to vet a person or group who wants to minister in the institution. A chaplain may not be of your religious faith, but they most often are intent on being fair in setting time and space for inmates of that faith to participate.

Let me explain some things about programming. The decision to schedule a group program or a volunteer is based on the number of people incarcerated of that faith, not the desire of various outside faith groups wanting to come in. In prisons, if a denomination wishes to come in for a service, and there are enough inmates from that group to rationally provide that service to those of that faith, it is announced denominationally, but anyone may attend, even non-Christian religious inmates. The fact is many protestant Christian inmates are fine attending a generic "Protestant Christian" service and focus on the common ground of the gospel of Jesus Christ. Inmates just want to come together to have corporate worship. And there are some who also come just to get out of their cells. Point being, that inmate complaining to you may be working from a far different motive than religious zeal. Keep that in mind before you hit up a chaplain with a complaint an inmate has brought to you.

Protestant volunteers and groups are easier to find and schedule because it's in their history and practice. Bottom line is they just have more volunteers. But even in that dynamic, it can get more complicated. Some Christian groups believe only their beliefs are correct and refuse dogmatically to generically worship with other denominations. They have even gone to court and won the right to have *separate services* with their label in prisons making parity in scheduling tedious. Can you imagine, with all the branches of the protestant faith groups, if all insisted on parity in separate worship times with their denominational label, just how few and far between those services would be? So, the perspective of outside groups to what is fair is sometimes lacking when it comes to scheduling in jails and prisons. What may seem unfair is simply a practical approach to scheduling.

Unfortunately, sometimes, a relationship of tension between a chaplain and a volunteer trickles down to inmates who then try to pit the volunteer against the system and/or the chaplain. They try to pull in the volunteer by implying they are being mistreated unfairly in religious programming. This happens particularly around ceremonial times of various religions.

When an inmate is processed, they are asked if they have a religion. It is noted in their file. While religious programs are usually open to anyone, including inmates just exploring religions, the exception to that rule is where changes in institutional time frames or ceremonial foods come into play. Participation in those events is usually limited to the inmates declared religion during an established timeline. This applies to many non-Christian religions, and those inmates have become pretty well practiced in crying wolf to their outside clergy volunteers and representatives. A chaplain has to budget for the ceremonial items and work out prayer times that might not fall into standard operating times of the institution. Continuous changes to a participation list can cause chaos. Inmates tend to play religious roulette during these times, changing from religion to religion so they can be part of the group getting special foods and prayer times. There's not too much in prison that individualizes, and being part of a group that has mandated holy day observances is a draw for some inmates. When their participation is denied as a fly-by-night opportunist during ceremonial events, that's when inmates will try to involve a volunteer to intercede by claiming bias on the part of the chaplain. Inmates know they have to be of a faith to participate in ceremonial foods and altered hours for prayer times. So, don't be pulled into friction between a chaplain and an inmate over things like that.

Even with the explanations, some volunteers insist on feeling persecuted and get a little touchy and even mistrustful of the fairness of a chaplain not of their faith. There was an older gentleman not of my denomination that caused a scene in the lobby when I was checking him in. He was always on the verge of being offended on behalf of his group. On this particular day, I was the only chaplain on duty. When I met him in the lobby to be escorted in, he wanted to bring in grape juice and wafers for his denominational mandatory weekly communion service because another chaplain had told him supplies had not been ordered in time. He claimed the other chaplain had approved him bringing them in. The glitch was no one had told me, and there was no memo. Allowing liquids and food items into a prison without verification isn't done for obvious reasons. When I questioned him regarding bringing such items in without prior proper documentation, he became defensive and indignant, claiming all sorts of bias. The man was supposed to wear hearing aids but never wore them to the prison, which complicated his ability to hear the questions I was asking and explanations I was giving. I always had to raise my voice for him to hear me each time he came in. After some discussion and permission from the duty lieutenant to cover my tail on allowing the items in, I let him bring in the items.

But, apparently, that wasn't good enough for him. He called the associate warden the next day and complained that I was disrespectful. A lobby officer who witnessed the interaction and was questioned during the investigation had reported I had raised my voice in the lobby at the volunteer, which, of course, I had because the guy didn't wear his hearing aids. I was about to be written up for bad communication with the public. The person looking into the complaint had never even asked me what had occurred. I wasn't having it. I called the associate warden and clarified the events. The tide turned in my favor. She backed me up for being so careful about nonapproved items coming in and recognized the older man was just being overzealous.

The volunteer forgot why he was there and brought more tension to an already tense place by perceiving me as an adversary against his religious practice rather than tending to guidelines that in the bigger picture actually protected his ability to even come into the institution. You see, there's always some inside information or rule a volunteer doesn't understand. But because of public perception and the political nature of dealing with the public, I had been put through an investigation for just doing my job.

Let me throw in this oddity that sometimes happens between religious groups. These topics tend to flush rabbits, but it's important you know this. Be careful not to be pulled into inmate mentality of the religious *equality* card. Specifically, one religion may have mandated events that require special times and foods, while the faith you represent does not. Inmates may approach you to insist they get provided a special group meal just to be "fair." Just because one faith may have special ceremonial celebrations requiring liturgical symbolic food items does not call for the *creation* of an equitable celebration in a faith that does not.

For example, Jewish inmates have Passover, and some prisons will accommodate specific ceremonies that include special foods. Muslims in prison have the month of Ramadan, which mandates they fast during the day and eat only after dark. Ramadan ends in a ceremonial meal. These are mandates of their faith, and where it's possible, many federal and state prisons accommodate.

But, believe it or not, a lot of complaints come from the many Christian religions that do not have *mandated* ceremonies that require special foods. They often pull the *it's-not-fair* complaint.

They want their *special* meal. Here's where a teaching moment comes in. Volunteers can teach them to be grounded in their own faith. It's your responsibility as a volunteer to address the principles of *your* faith and encourage them not to play the "it's not fair" game.

I hope you can see just how complex the role of chaplain is and seek to have the best relationship possible with them. Work with your chaplains, not against them.

CHAPTER 7

Managing Religion in Jails and Prisons

Don't get insulted by my usage of the phrase *managing religion.* Remember: I'm trying to give you information on how jails and prisons run so you can minister as wisely and as unfettered as possible. Facilitating religious practice in jails in prisons is just that—management. The bottom line for administrators is not about making judgments regarding the *truth* of a religion but trying to find a way that inmates can practice their faith without causing any security concerns.

When the founders wrote the first amendment, they had come out of a history of government having one state-sanctioned religion. This amendment was essentially their best effort to tell the government to stay out of the individual's right to determine whether to worship God or how to go about that worship. Our founders said to butt out in *any* way except to preserve our right to worship as we please. The Founding Fathers wrote the Constitution also assuming common sense would still exist through the ages and that the original intent of the amendment protecting religious freedom would stay the foundation. Nope, didn't happen. Common sense takes quite a beating when it comes to religious requests in jails and prisons. The first amendment applies to inmates too, and, believe me, they know it and use religion to push back at the system, making some of the most outrageous demands to push at the system. Some will file lawsuits before their request is even studied. A person who has never worked the inside of one of these places really has no clue how an inmate who wants to practice their faith can impact the security and smooth running of an institution. Corrections staff wrestle with strange religious issues all the time. This can get pretty bizarre.

I once had to confiscate a dead raccoon a camp inmate had found and had fashioned into a "medicine pouch." Chapel staff and the warden had quite a laugh at that one especially when trying to determine how to dispose of it. To inmates, such items are sacred, and although it may be unauthorized, the discarding of such confiscated items can blow up in your face publicly if not handled right. The warden let the completely intact, perfectly taxidermied raccoon sit in his chair while we discussed it. I ended up calling a tribal representative to come get it, and that satisfied the inmate. After all was said and done, we all got a good laugh, and I ended up with the nickname Dances with Raccoons.

If you think that was bizarre, another inmate had dead bugs taped to his locker, claiming they were his religious sacrifices. The corrections officer was probably startled by the bug motif when he opened the inmate's locker during a shakedown. I was called to the unit to deal with the matter. Even the inmate couldn't come up with a valid religious reason for his choice of worship. The bugs came down.

And still another had a makeshift altar by his bed where he'd place food offerings daily. In the free world, his religion practiced food offerings, but, apparently, his gods didn't like his food choices while he was locked up and didn't partake, leaving the food rotting in his cell. All these items were self-created for religious expression and had some merit in his religion's culture but posed hygiene issues, including smelly rotting food inviting gnats, ants, and roaches. That gave reason to override this particular practice of his faith and have him discard the perishable foods. Inmates are allowed to have religious items but only those acquired through proper channels and stored properly in their lockers.

One chaplain, after checking with a non-Christian groups outside clergy regarding disposal of literature, was cleaning out some age-old periodicals of that denomination to make room for new literature from his faith and made the unfortunate decision to cart it to the rear gate during an inmate move. An inmate from that faith saw it and threw himself across the cart, screaming it was *holy literature.* He wouldn't budge and was making a scene as though the chaplain was kicking his dog. No matter this inmate never graced the chapel or read anything religious except during his high holy days where special foods were involved. The chaplain just sighed and turned around, carting it back to the chapel, and disposed of it later. Lesson learned, I suppose.

Management even filters down to attempted lessons on stealing in the inmate restroom. A shortage of toilet paper in the institution resulted in units rationing rolls to two per week per inmate. All of a sudden, toilet paper was a hot commodity. The chapel was hit so hard with toilet paper thefts from the inmate chapel restroom that I had a sign made and posted right above the toilet paper dispenser that read "Thou shalt not steal." I was sure that play on a person's conscience would work for any religion. Silly me. I was doing my end-of-day security check of all the rooms in the chapel before locking up for the day. Figuring the sign had worked, I checked the inmate restroom and found not only rolls of toilet paper had been stolen but the sign too. I laugh about that to this day.

The management of the practice of religion can bring a few laughs as you can tell, but it is also incredibly political. Ironically, inmates seem to have more rights religiously than does the ordinary citizen in the free world. People are quicker to champion an inmate who accuses the system of violating their religious rights while in prison because they are perceived by the public as helpless to fight the monstrosity that is the government. That puts the warden and staff in the spotlight. Not only is it costly when lawsuits are filed, but even an accusation by an inmate that they are being kept from practicing their religion can be a stain on a career regardless of the truth of the matter. No warden wants to be labeled as violating an inmate's religious rights. As a result, accusations against the system are vigorously investigated, and staff often feel like they have been put through the wringer by the inmate and the system on something that should be a matter of common sense in application. Responding to religious complaints can perpetuate an adversarial role and be costly to the system that routinely has to fight the many lawsuits from inmates pushing at the system using religion as a weapon.

The reality is secular institutions and religion will never mesh. One is sterile; the other, abstract. The way an individual interprets their faith and wishes to apply that while locked up is going to, of necessity, be altered because of the nature of the security environment and regimentation of their living situation. You think it's hard dealing with religious issues that arise in the free world? Just try managing religion in jails and prisons in a forum filled with dysfunctional people all intent on manipulating the system. So, all we can hope for is to manage, within the secular, individual inmate's religious rights as well as all the competing religions vying for time, space, and a full measure of practice even while incarcerated.

Yes, it can be pretty interesting managing religion in prisons and jails. Sometimes, it boils down to a judgment call by staff after looking at the big picture for the whole institution. As a volunteer or new chaplain, keep that in mind.

CHAPTER 8

Be Security Conscious

The places that house society's criminals have one mission at the top of their list: security. Be security conscious. This is the number-one cardinal rule when ministering in jails and prisons. Everything else is down on the list technically. We know what can change the lives of the incarcerated, and that's why the gospel is brought into these dark places. However, the mission of jails and prisons is not about you bringing the gospel of salvation or encouragement to the lost. It's a very sterile mission. It's about keeping the lawbreakers locked up until they have their day in court or serve out their time.

While dealing with civilians coming in to do various types of programming is part of the job, facilitating volunteers is sometimes seen as a necessary evil. Civilians entering into the belly of the beast become liabilities and are often unwelcome interruptions to the smooth running of the institution. If correctional officers know you are security conscious and follow the rules, it reduces their concern that you are going to become a casualty of a breach of security in some way. That goes a long way for you being able to minister freely in the prison or jail environment.

I'm not going to try to go into all applications of security, but I will give you an easy to remember foundational rule. If you don't know you can, don't. Don't take anything from them, and don't give anything to them that has not been approved. You'll be given guidelines for dos and don'ts for volunteering in your facility. Follow them. Violations of contraband regulations may end your ability to visit ever again and end up actually causing someone to be hurt or even aid in an escape.

Most people think of contraband as the big stuff, like drugs or weapons. Contraband can be anything, from handing the inmate a pen to bringing in a magazine or letter for an inmate. A letter, a pen, a magazine? How would any of those things create a security issue? I chose those common items as examples just to show you nothing can be taken for granted when ministering in a secure facility. When I say inmates can fashion a weapon from anything, I'm not joking. Even plastic spoons or toothbrushes have been used to fashion weapons, so don't casually minimize even handing an inmate a pen. Pens have been used as an easy weapon to take out the eye of staff or inmate. The hollow pens can be used as tattoo instruments or a place to hide drugs. Even those small half pencils have been misused by inmates to get attention. How? What better way to get a trip out of the jail to the local hospital than to swallow a pencil. Inmates bent on forcing a trip to the outside ER have even swallowed Sporks, those combination plastic spoon forks. They can't ban everything, of course, but the point is inmates can fashion weapons from anything. They are incredibly creative.

I'll give an illustration on an innocent everyday action from when I first started as a chaplain intern in a county jail. One of my rounds was to segregation where you might have people separated for any number of reasons from fighting to observation for mental health issues. I was careful to only pass out paperback books and other paper literature. I received a call from the segregation officer a few hours later after rounds that one inmate had removed staples from one of the small devotional pamphlets and had inserted them under her eyelids. Yes. Her eyelids. Quit laughing! Who would have thought, right? And distribution of literature in segregation was an ordinary thing. You just never know who you are dealing with. So, think about what you are doing even to the absurd.

It works in reverse too. Taking things from inmates can breach security too. Never take anything from an inmate to take out of the prison or jail. No gift of art from an inmate or a card of thanks should ever be taken without prior approval for accountability. No story of slow mail or no stamps or some legal issue should ever make you do that. While the request may be seem benign to you, it may actually be an inmate tying to circumvent a sanction against him for breaking a rule, or he may be testing you to see how naïve you are so they can manipulate you to do something more egregious. Do you want to be responsible for delivering a letter to an inmate's victim, effectively harassing and intimidating a witness or victim of his crime? Even transferring a verbal message to their family member on the outside may get someone killed or set up some code for a drug deal. All outgoing and incoming phone calls and mail are monitored, so don't get in the middle of that. Again, you don't know the history of the person you are talking to. These examples may be a bit extreme, but the point is, whatever the rules are, follow them. Think outside the box on what an infraction of the rules may cause. If you don't know you can, don't.

Here's another key rule. If you have a question about something, *ask staff, not the inmate,* what you can give or take out. That's important. Inmates will manipulate. They are trying to survive emotionally and physically. Yes, they will manipulate even a pastor or layman coming in to deal with them spiritually. They will tell you a half-truth to get you to do them a favor, purposefully or as an extension of a life already confused and out of control. If you take the bait, you have just been demoted from spiritual advisor to gopher or middleman for some scheme.

Keep in mind the inmates are given a handbook when they first arrive and are responsible for knowing the rules. Inmates often know the volunteer rules better than you do and have no problem in manipulating you to bend them. Even approved items that seem insignificant to security, which includes making sure the well-being of inmates are protected, can be the object of harm or manipulation. Be security conscious. Follow the rules. Remember your mission. Go home. If you don't know you can, *don't.*

CHAPTER 9

Volunteers and Safety Issues

I know it's blunt, but it has to be said. Chaplains and religious volunteers bleed too. Jails and prisons are dangerous places. You're coming into an environment with hundreds of dysfunctional, emotionally charged, angry people who are trying to survive. They need help, and some want help. But their emotions can boil over any moment in a variety of ways. Be fully aware that every time you come in to minister, there is potential for some violent act upon you. That's in spite of safeguards and emergency plans in place for protection of civilians and staff for anything that might go down in the institution. It's important you take that seriously and always have situational awareness.

The staff that are tasked with keeping inmates locked up are constantly aware that a quiet unit can explode in moments, inmate on inmate or inmate on staff. Staff will do what they have to do to survive in the moment while perhaps trying to protect an inmate being butchered by another. There's always the stressor in the back of their mind. Those decisions made in the moment may allow survival but later may be politicized and put the staff on the hot seat that may cost their jobs. Corrections officers, as law enforcement, have seen things no one should have to see. Their training includes documented incidents and including horrific videos where staff couldn't enter a unit until backup arrived, and they had to stand outside while watching an inmate stab another inmate over and over who didn't care who was watching. It also includes documentation of staff being attacked or murdered by inmates. This is why corrections staff often wish religious volunteers would stick to civilian church on the outside. Every time a volunteer enters this workplace, it's another person they have to protect in some fashion if something should kick off. If you get hurt, the publicity would be disastrous.

Some of you are probably skeptical an inmate would ever hurt a religious volunteer. You are just sure God will protect you. If you're that naïve, then jail and prison ministry isn't for you. Reality check. The Bible is full of martyrs. Pray for protection, but God didn't make you stupid. Pay attention to your environment. In jails and prisons, it doesn't take much to spark violence.

I'm about to give a few examples. Keep in mind: my personal examples are minuscule compared to what corrections staff have experienced, but these examples show that there's always that one inmate or group of inmates who do not respect your role of spiritual advisor and may bring harm to you. This is not intended to scare you away from ministry in jails and prisons but make you wise in that ministry. If they will potentially harm chaplains who are spiritual shepherds in the jails and prisons, what makes you think they wouldn't harm you as a religious volunteer?

1. I was supervising afternoon programming with several volunteers inside the chapel. My chapel orderly alerted me to a situation in the middle of the compound. I looked

out the window, and two gangs had squared off on the compound. There were probably several hundred.

The alert went out to staff, and units were locked down. I separated my volunteers from inmates who were participating in religious programming. I locked the inmates in the larger chapel area while pulling the volunteers into the chapel office. Inmates attending the religious programming could have been part of a bigger plan to take that part of the institution and take hostages in a planned event. One wrong word or movement by the inmates on the compound would spark a full-scale brawl that could move to many parts of the institution. My duty was to protect the volunteers as well as secure the chapel inmates for our protection and theirs. No one was going anywhere.

I watched events unfolding from the chapel window. Then the captain and a couple of his lieutenants walked into the middle of the compound and stood courageously between the two groups. He was either foolhardy or depending on his established rapport with the inmates. I don't know what was said, but after about fifteen minutes, the inmates began to disperse back to their units. After calling Control and getting permission, I allowed the chapel inmates to return to their units and escorted the volunteers out. The volunteers really had no clue how badly this could have gotten in a flash.

2. It was a Friday afternoon, and the Muslims were having their Jum'ah prayer in the main chapel auditorium attended by about fifty Muslim inmates. It was close to their holy days of fasting during Ramadan. There are

deadlines inmates have to adhere to regarding placing their names on participation. There are often many deviations of institution mealtime time frames during various religious holy days. The amount of inmates participating demands deadlines for participation for organization with food service and other things requiring deadlines to be strictly followed. Constantly updating a list for the units of participating inmates leads to confusion for both unit COs and food service staff.

One inmate had come to me wanting to get on the list after a deadline had past. He was denied. He entered angrily into the Muslim meeting and stirred up the group with several lies, claiming he was being targeted unfairly as a Muslim. I had come out of the chapel office and into the chapel lobby in anticipation of the hourly move to be called when out surged dozens of inmates who surrounded me. Their group leaders began to complain and voice their disproval of my decision.

Get the dynamics here: I was one chaplain working the chapel alone surrounded by dozens of hostile male inmates. One wrong word, and I was history. No doubt God protected me and gave me wisdom. I had the presence of mind to stand firm and tell them they had a choice: they could all spend their holy days locked in segregation for causing a disturbance in the chapel all over the lies of one of their members, or their leaders could come talk to me later in my office for resolution. They chose the latter and stood down and moved on out the door to their units.

I later learned the chapel cameras in control had locked in on the situation, saw my hand on my radio, and were just waiting to send the cavalry should I make that call. The corrections angels had my back, but I'm not sure if they could have sent help in time to keep me from a sound beating.

3. Another time, I was working the chapel, and a fellow chaplain said he was leaving the chapel area and to be aware that one of the mental health inmates had threatened to come back on the next move and kill him. I remember looking at him with a skeptical smile, thinking he was kidding. Why would he be leaving the area with me holding the bag if he hadn't taken care of the issue? Figuring he had reported the inmate to the mental health unit and the shift lieutenant, I thought no more about it.

   On the next move, an inmate walked in the outer office area and asked for the other chaplain, announcing that God had told him to kill that chaplain. He said he didn't have much time because he'd been told not to come over to the chapel again today and to stay in the unit. I was virtually alone with a crazy man intent on wreaking havoc on the other chaplain that had offended him. I was thinking maybe any chaplain would fill the bill for his mandate from God.

   Again, the Lord gave me presence of mind. I pretended interest in his mission and allowed him to explain why he was so angry with the other chaplain. But my mind was going ninety to nothing trying to figure out how to get the inmate out of the chapel before

I became a substitute for the other chaplain. I had a desk between him and me, but he was inadvertently blocking my exit out of the office. I remember interrupting him lightheartedly with concern in my voice for him. I said, "Oh my. You know what? The move is almost over, and didn't you tell me you weren't supposed to leave the unit? I know you don't want to get caught out of your unit and get in trouble. Come on! Let me walk you back so you won't get in trouble. Let's hurry!" I moved toward the door, and he moved out of the way and followed, still berating the other chaplain. I succeeded in getting him back to the mental health unit right before the move ended.

When I got back to the chapel, I called his unit. They were very apologetic he'd made it to the chapel because the other chaplain had called and alerted them about his threat. Someone had dropped the ball about monitoring him on the move and had put my safety on the line. Moral? Be prepared for anything. But even then, it's only God's angels that protect you.

4. Religious issues in prisons and jails can get tense pretty quickly if a member of a branch of religion thinks they are being treated unfairly. Inmates sometimes form variations of a benign religion, adding a racist tenant to it. This is to have their gang meetings in the chapel in the name of religion. One such group had added a strong-armed salute and a swastika to a pagan faith. They knew this was prohibited in prison. No matter what they claimed the gesture meant to them, historically, it was seen as Nazi Aryan practices. I caught them engaging

in the salute one day and shut down their meeting on the spot.

In their view, I had humiliated them as a group, so, to them, I had to be punished. I was on to their fake practices that were no more than a cover-up for their white supremacy gang meetings, and I was in their way. They devised an odd scheme of revenge to use aids blood to make me sick. They tried intimidating an inmate chapel worker to either put it in my coffee or put a tainted needle in my chair. That inmate dropped a kite—inmate slang for a written note—to let the lieutenant know about the plan. The inmates were placed in segregation and ultimately transferred to another facility.

By the way, that was the penny version of a very detailed interesting plot. I will say both methods of infecting me wouldn't have worked anyway, since inmates aren't allowed in our offices without supervision, not even when cleaning the offices, and I never had an inmate make me coffee or be anywhere near any drink I was consuming.

5. It was standard practice to have chapel workers hang back after end-of-day programming to clean the chapel after the last move from the chapel and before final recall. Once they were gone, I'd do my security checks of the bathrooms and other rooms to make sure everyone was gone, lock inner doors, and make sure things were secure. One evening, I was sending the last few inmates across the compound when an inmate worker silently mouthed to me a warning there was an inmate who

was not a chapel worker hanging back in the restroom. The implication was he was waiting for me to clear the bathroom for his own vile reasons. I left the chapel outer door open and asked the compound officer to step over to the chapel. Standing in the open exit door, I ordered the inmate to leave the bathroom while making sure I was nowhere near it. The compound officer arrived as the inmate was leaving the restroom. The inmate hurried out the door with the explanation he hadn't expected to be in the bathroom so long. I told the officer my suspicions about the inmate's motive as we watched him scurry across the compound, and we gave each other knowing glances. Though the inmate's motives couldn't be proven, I was relieved I was able to divert a potential attack without incident. While you don't want to overtly rely on inmates to watch your back, they often do without your endorsement. This time, I was thankful. Angels come in many forms.

6. I was notified one day by the shift lieutenant that an inmate had been locked up after a shakedown of his locker. It seems a takeover plot of the institution was exposed by a list that was found. Besides plans for the takeover, staff was ranked by threat to the accomplishment of this plan because of that particular staff member's awareness of security and willingness to make them follow the rules and behave. Some staff were in the category of limited threat, a high-watch level, and those they needed to eliminate right off the bat for the plan to take place. My rank? I was on the elimination list. I didn't know whether to feel gratified they were aware

I was security conscious and held them to personal responsibility, or sad they had continued to carry on in their rebellious behavior in spite of the fact they could use their prison experience to make a U-turn in their lives. Regardless, my point is even religious people who care about their souls can be seen as a threat to some inmates. Some people just don't have any intentions of changing their lives. Remember: they crucified Christ.

7. Not all incidents are complex. You never know what is going to set off someone. An inmate sucker punched one of my fellow chaplains in the mouth when he simply said no to his request for something.

Before I scare some of you off, let me emphasize that these incidents are rare statistically toward chaplains, and even less for religious volunteers. Those few inmates who might harm a spiritual advisor have to consider double whammy repercussions. One, they would be sanctioned by the system, including more time; and, two, inmates who frequent the chapel would render inmate justice on that inmate or group who would harm a chaplain or religious volunteer. Most inmates respect your mission regardless of whether they agree with your particular brand of religion. But dissing a religious volunteer is considered major disrespect. You don't want to make a habit of allowing inmates to protect you, but many are watching your back. They even do that for officers. Not every person incarcerated is a raging bull. But, again, never rely on inmates for your protection.

Those examples should alert you to the possibility of that one inmate who really doesn't respect anything, you included.

If they can make some statement by harming you, they just might chance it and accept the consequences. Be fully aware of the potential for harm when coming into a jail or prison. Determine if you are willing to accept some level of risk, and don't blame the alligator if it does what is basic to an alligator's nature. Be aware.

As an endnote on this subject, if you are feeling uneasy about something, don't be embarrassed to let staff know even if it turns out to be nothing. Gut feelings are a gift from God, and you don't have to be ashamed or feel weak about sharing your concern about an inmate or situation that may be causing you concern for your safety.

CHAPTER 10

Don't Get Comfortable

This chapter goes down a different path from the last chapters on security and safety. It's in the same family, and the subject deserves some attention. I think it's at the root of breaches of security by volunteers. They just get too comfortable. Volunteers often asked me if I ever got scared working with all the convicts. My standard answer was that I have a healthy caution but not fear. I never forgot where I worked and ministered with eyes wide open. Scripture says Jesus knew what was in the heart of men and didn't put his trust in them. That's the sweet spot for volunteers to remember.

If you are called to work with inmates, initially, there will be a natural anxiety, but, eventually, you'll start to become familiar with the environment. It's inevitable after a time of volunteering in jails or prisons that a person may be lulled into a sense of ease because of the familiarity and routine, and you will find yourself letting your guard down. But let me warn you: don't get comfortable. I'm talking about the type of comfort that you might have in your free world church. Jails and prisons are not your church. A feeling of comfort is not what you are looking for when coming into a jail or prison.

It's okay to have a measure of discomfort. Don't see your discomfort as a sign you aren't trusting God. Feeling uncomfortable is not a lack of faith. Your comfort must be redefined as total dependency on God in your mission, not the absence of fear or anxiety or due diligence. Those feelings make you more alert to your surroundings.

Many of our tasks as servants of God take us into places where we'd rather not go, dealing with people we'd rather not be around. But, face it: that's where the mission is. Anyone can minister within the confines of church walls and fellowship of the saints in our own comfort zones. We get pretty good at casting out the line from the bank and reeling them in with events scheduled at our churches. That's our comfort zone. But being on mission means we go where the lost and drowning are, and that means pushing out from the bank and being willing to go where the Lord sends us, engaging in true servant leader sacrifice to accomplish the purpose of the Lord in each situation. Servant leaders don't have to have a feeling of comfort to be empowered to fulfill their role in what God is doing in someone else's crisis. God is doing His work of revealing Himself with people in crisis. As God's people, our responsibility is to be in relationship with Him, so we're prepared when called upon to enter the crisis of another with the presence of God. Don't seek a feeling or try to *get* comfortable in your mission. Let God help you to be or at ease as you place your trust in Him in the midst of your ministry. It's a defined Psalm 37 comfort where we rest in the Lord and trust in Him.

Please hear me on this subject of comfort. Your comfort can lead to presumption. This is a big trap for volunteers. I want to get the attention of anyone who is resisting what I'm saying.

You are the one who is heading for a fall. You may be one who has no fear of the prison environment, confident in your ability to work with inmates and officers, and be well versed in scripture. Take heed. Pride goes before a fall. Scripture shows time and again that God's most dedicated people who knew the principles and had relationship with God were susceptible to being diverted to putting confidence in their own abilities. This often results in unconsciously trying to be all things to all people and actually watering down the message for the purpose of maintaining a fan base with their inmate group rather than bringing the hard principles of life to them and risking rejection.

A war story is necessary to emphasize how serious this is. I had a jail volunteer once who had been volunteering for quite some time. He was a sweet guy that just wanted to serve the Lord and reach out to people. He was good at relating to all types of people, including the families of the inmates. On his way into the jail one day, he encountered a family of an inmate coming to leave money for the inmate's commissary needs. He got into conversation with the family in the lobby of the jail, and the family told him the control officer had rejected a Christian magazine they had wanted to leave for him. They said they wanted their relative to have it for his spiritual growth and, seeing this volunteer as friendly, succeeded in getting him to agree to take the magazine to the inmate. The volunteer, though familiar with the all the rules about taking things from inmates or giving anything to them without approval from the chaplain, decided it was okay to take the magazine. He was familiar with the magazine and knew it to teach Christian core principles. This was something he reasoned this inmate needed to read.

He added the magazine to his own approved items and passed through the control doors.

However, the control entry officer had seen the encounter, and once the volunteer was in the secure area, he asked to see what the family had handed him. The control officer, who had already denied the family leaving the magazine, decided to check the magazine out, as was his duty. When the officer opened the magazine, he found marijuana folded between the pages. Boom! Just like that, the well-earned credibility of this volunteer went down the tubes. He was dismissed from the program, all because he presumed the authority to disregard the rules by which he had promised to abide.

What reasoning had gone through his mind? Was he a paid employee of the jail? Had the rules suddenly changed because of a sob story from a family tugging on his heart? The action of the volunteer was not ministry. It was nothing more than a presumptuous spirit. He had gotten too comfortable in his role, and it translated to a subtle pride that had caused him to give himself permission to alter a rule. Even as a staff chaplain, I was very sure to consult and keep correctional staff and supervisors in the loop by memo regarding items I was bringing into the jail or prison for inmate religious use. Shun the very appearance of evil was my motto.

Listen! When you get too comfortable, it's about you. It's like Peter, who, when he kept his eyes on the Lord, was able to walk on water, but when he looked to his feet standing on liquid, something no human should be able to do, he sank. Same principle. Jail and prison ministry is a lot like walking on water in a storm looking at Jesus. You have to remember: every time you enter the walls, you are on mission for God. If you take your eyes off the real authority and rationalize a permission regarding a rule, you'll fall into the trap of presumption and pride, and I guarantee you, you will sink. Rules exist for order and security. If you get comfortable, and it translates to you bending rules for spiritual reasons, you've fallen into a trap, and it's time for you to become accountable to the authorities over you or minister elsewhere. Whenever you fall, you damage the ministry of other volunteers as a consequence, bringing them under harsher scrutiny by jail officials.

A common way volunteers get too comfortable is engaging in exchanging personal information with inmates. Being casually friendly but not detailed is the key. It's hard not to share about your children and your vacations or your next mission trip with your church, even the kind of pets you have, but if you are engaging in that type of conversation, you're getting too chummy. They don't need your personal life details. They don't need to know your dog's name or what you feed him. Inmates try to find personal information they can use to get to know you better, some with genuine benign interest but others with malicious intent to bait you. If you like dogs, horses, a vacation spot, they try to make some connection to you so they can experience your life and perhaps dream a little. But unchecked conversation can breed familiarity and lead you to trouble.

Even well-meaning inmates can get you in trouble. One volunteer shared that her church was about to go on a mission trip and were raising funds to do so. The inmate asked if he could contribute, and in a moment of overzealousness, the volunteer shared her address. The inmate called his family and asked them to contribute to the mission since the volunteer had been so kind to him. They sent a nice check to the volunteer for the mission trip. She had thought no more of it until she received the check, and then she panicked, realizing she had violated a guideline. She called me, which, of course, was the right thing to do. I had to bring it to the attention of the administration, and after some discussion, she was told to return the money. However, she was also suspended temporarily from the program with the reinstatement requirement of a refresher course in the rules. She had no idea at the time she could have been permanently prohibited from volunteering there. Her main mistake was sharing too much information with the inmate.

Even chaplains can stumble by getting too comfortable, so don't think you can't be baited. One chaplain casually shared about his financial woes and his kid's money problems. Unbelievable as it sounds, that inmate-staff relationship evolved to where the chaplain was talked into bringing in contraband for the inmate in exchange for the inmate's family helping the chaplain's kid pay his school fees. He was fired. So, again, remember your mission, and always be aware jails and prisons are your ministry, not your church. Know your place in that role, and don't get comfortable. It can lead to a presumptuous spirit.

CHAPTER 11

Go with the Right Attitude

The most important thing you take with you when volunteering in jails and prisons is surprisingly simple—it's a good attitude. If you can't bring that with you, all your knowledge of scripture and dedication is just so much hot air. So, check your heart when pondering if jail and prison ministry is your calling.

I don't know whether it's a case of pride or anxiety with some volunteers, but I've been chewed out many times by some of the most so-called dedicated of God's people. Sadly, it happens too frequently. Why would someone check their manners at the door? I'm sure they never intentionally planned to use a chaplain or correctional staff as an emotional dumping ground, but it happens more often than you'd believe. I've given them the benefit of the doubt by thinking an environment as unfamiliar as a jail or prison just unsettles some people who then give themselves permission to act out.

One question to ask yourself before you begin is, Why do I want to minister in a correctional environment? Is it your calling? Or do you have other reasons or maybe some personal biases? Maybe you have a personality that empathizes with those in pain, and you are on the outside looking in. For whatever reason, some volunteers already have some kind of chip on their shoulder and have an us-against-them attitude in mind for their ministry.

Several factors may impact attitude as a volunteer. Maybe some choose correctional ministries because they have had bad encounters with law enforcement that soured them in some way. Some even put their social justice mentality ahead of sharing the gospel. They see prison ministry as an opportunity to be a buffer for the downtrodden in some way. Or maybe they had a person in their family incarcerated. That certainly sparks some compassion for the incarcerated. Or maybe they've always been fascinated with law enforcement and watch too many cop shows.

More subtle areas impact your attitude. In your church, you may receive the respect due an elder, teacher, or pastor, and you may have unintentionally bought into whatever people are saying about you and expect respect. Flattery is fine. It's most often people trying to say thank you for blessing them. However, putting flattery in the right perspective is important, or other seeds sprout that can affect your attitude, some being arrogance, entitlement, unrealistic expectations, and plain old pride.

You may have held a role of authority and position in your church but have been sidelined for some reason. You may see the prison as an opportunity to use your spiritual gifts again. There's certainly nothing wrong with that. Maybe you see it as your own personal mission field as an extension of your church. After all, admittedly, jail and prison ministry is not for everyone and holds some intrigue for those not called to it. It's an honor to be given the title of the church's prison minister. I get it. It should be respected as part of the whole mission of the church as surely as youth ministry, children's ministry, senior adult ministry, singles ministry, women's and men's ministry, and outreach to foreign and home missions. A church that ignores the ministry to the incarcerated, in whatever form that takes, has missed a segment of ministry to their local community that Jesus specifically addressed as important. I can't tell you how many times I have encountered leaders of churches who didn't even know there was a prison in their vicinity and have totally ignored their local and county jails. So, if jail and prison ministry is your calling, make sure your church is plugged into that. Your calling is important. People volunteering in jails or prisons for any other reason but that it's a calling will inadvertently increase the likelihood of a festering friction that may come out on staff when coming into a correctional facility.

When volunteers who have questionable motives come for a visit at the prison or jail, they give themselves permission to be rude and become demanding to chaplains, correctional officers, and sometimes even advocate for families in the lobby. I have to be quite frank with you here with no intent to be sarcastic. Reality check: these places are not sitting around waiting for you to arrive. Your congregational friends and family may value your ministry, but a jail or prison is not your church. And if you are mixing some social justice issue in your ministry, attributing it to a perverted concept of the mission of Jesus himself, you are really missing the point. It's your mission field. Missionaries who succeed go into an environment aware of the culture just as Jesus did and ministered with understanding and wisdom and with the foundational eternal mission of Christ as the plumb line. You'd do better to remember the simplicity that is in Christ with the goal of presenting the gospel of salvation. A relationship with Christ is the starting point for changing anything wrong in our society, not a sterile social justice approach. Change happens when the heart changes, not the other way around.

I've had some pretty bad experiences with this type of person. A pastor visited a jail where I was director of chaplains. At this facility, the chaplains were tasked with the responsibility of doing an initial credential check before the deputy proceeded with running the driver's license for the background check. This was a large facility housing four thousand inmates. You can imagine the hubbub of the place. A correctional facility has priorities. Ministerial visits, while expected and sanctioned, are not at the top of the list. When I was called to validate the credentials of this minister, it took me a bit of time to get to the lobby to perform this function. In an eleven-story building, you don't just skip down the hall and out the door. This pastor had shown up unannounced, so whatever I was occupied with had to be interrupted. My office was behind security areas, so I was subject to electronically controlled doors and elevators to get down to the lobby.

When I approached the minister, a senior pastor of a large church, he was noticeably agitated, pacing and looking at his watch. When I asked for his credential, he let me have it, and I don't mean his credentials. Why did I make him wait? Didn't I know he was a busy man? He was a taxpayer, and the mayor and sheriff would hear about this. I tried to find a break in his tirade to explain how the jail functioned, as well as why it had taken so long, but to no avail.

Now, I'm not known for being a mouse, but I restrained myself from going into my impression of Old Testament Moses striking the rock. This preacher needed a good smack on the noggin. I asked this pastor one thing: how would he like it if I came into his church and acted in the entitled manner he was acting? The example he was setting for the officers and those in the lobby was certainly not Christlike. I was treated to an example of why we should not cast our pearls before swine. He told me I was not a real minister and tore his driver's license from my hand and stomped out with the eyes of staff, inmate families, and mine, watching him leave. I must admit I was disappointed that he was walking so fast, my prayer calling for the door to hit him in the rear as he left was not honored. I was certainly no spiritually richer for having encountered him! I have talked to hardened criminals that were more polite.

I have many stories like that, unfortunately. Bottom line is, check your pride at the door. This is not about you. Prisons and jails are not your church. The people who work in these places are on mission too, and that mission is to keep those in conflict with society's laws locked away from you and me. That includes feeding, clothing exchanges, mail call, escorting inmates to court and attorney visits, and so much more. That's what they are doing 24-7. When you come into their house, things are simply not going to shut down for you no matter your schedule or place in the community. Keep in mind: you are not only there to minister to the inmate, but your presence has the opportunity to minister God's grace to the officers and staff of the institution as well as include inmate families you may meet in the lobby. And Lord knows even chaplains need the kind words of another Christian to bless their day.

I noticed a pattern with these Christian visitors who erupt upon chaplains and staff. Most all were in a hurry and were fitting the jail visit into their schedule. Time is a mitigating factor that affects our attitude. In a stress-filled occupation, dealing with staff, inmates, families, and dysfunction, I learned to make time my friend, not my enemy, by being flexible. This is especially important when you visit a correctional institution. Your trips to the jail or prison should not be a side errand you fit into your otherwise busy schedule. It should be your goal for the day. At least plan to be there for a few hours. This kind of ministry visit should not be treated with the same detached attitude you would have if you were just driving through the ATM at your bank. I don't mean you have to see your trip as all consuming, but I wouldn't have any deadlines to meet somewhere else later on. That will only add to your anxiety and perhaps cause you to act out in a manner you never would in your church. You don't know what's transpired that day at the jail. Don't set yourself up with false expectations that you are going to get in and out on time. Don't be in a hurry. Take your time, and be flexible. And, above all, bring a good attitude.

CHAPTER 12

Determine Your Level of Involvement

Is it ever appropriate for a volunteer with access to the jail or prison to get involved with material or legal needs of an inmate, including with family matters? Isn't it our responsibility to do more than just pray and counsel with them? The complicated answer is, yes, no, and maybe. Sorry. It's just not that universally easy to give an answer. But it does help to define your ministry and stick to it.

There are generally three applications of jail and prison ministry. One deals with providing programs inside an institution. Another deals with issues of inmate's families from the outside essentially apart from the inmate, and the third is in connection with the inmate and the inmate's reentry into the community. You can imagine tentacles from all three sometimes connect your ministry.

It's the lone wolf volunteer that gets into the weeds and delves into the inside out ministry that I want to address at this point. While you are volunteering *inside* an institution in spiritual programming, fulfill your mission to share the gospel and equip them with spiritual tools to help them grow in their relationship with God. Period. Other types of help are more safely done from the outside with an entirely different group unattached to you. In fact, if your ministry is on the inside, and you carry your mission outside the jail or prison on behalf of inmates with whom you've established ministry relationships, you've probably violated the guidelines.

I get it. Sometimes, you'll feel, if you don't tangibly help an inmate or his/her family, that it will somehow turn them from God. But that's a flawed perspective. It's not favors they need. You are not there to be an emotional painkiller for them or to rescue them from the consequences of their actions that may leave their family hurting economically or emotionally, but to point them to their own relationship with God. That's the best help you can give the inmate and ultimately their family. A personal relationship with Christ will give them the courage and stability to grow into a responsible family member. Giving them an emotional fix or some tangible bail out does not allow them to deal with the core problems that brought them to this point in their life. It just delivers them from consequences. Those fixes only postpone the inevitable recycling of the same old behaviors, which often have taken the form of manipulating the emotions of those around them to get some physical relief from their pain. God wants to give them a permanent fix built on relationship with Him without you in the middle. It's not what you do for them; it's what God does for them. I advise you to transfer the request for help other than your programming ministry inside the institution to agencies equipped to address that.

Even doing that could be a gray area. While recommending agencies or particular churches that provide family assistance is appropriate at times, that doesn't translate to you doing the legwork for them.

The best way to explain what not to do is to give a real life example. I had a very kind woman who worked as one of my volunteers in a large county jail. An inmate she had been spiritually mentoring for a few years was getting out and had no place to go. This volunteer decided to open her home to this lady until she could find a job and get on her feet. When the woman was released, she moved in with the volunteer. Things went well for a while. The way I found out about the arrangement was when the volunteer called me, lamenting that the woman had left, gotten back on the drugs, and robbed her house. She had taken a risk and learned a hard lesson.

So, where's the balance? It's not unusual for releasing inmates to at the least ask you for continued contact after release. If that doesn't violate your particular jail or prison guidelines, make sure you only give them the phone number of your church, and let them contact you that way. There are too many horror stories of well-meaning volunteers who extend help beyond the ministry in jails who have been robbed or harmed by someone who, while locked up, were strong but relapsed when released. Don't play with that. Be safe. There are no jail bars between you and them when they get out. Your church or other agencies, not you personally, should deal with those issues of housing or other help after they release. But the best thing to do is make a firm distinction in the types of jail and prison ministry before you start.

Unfortunately, there are always exceptions that can keep you confused. In the exception where your church has some connection with an incarcerated church member or a church member has a family member incarcerated, you as an approved ministry volunteer inside a jail or prison should *never* allow yourself to be a go-between for that process. I repeat, if your church chooses to assist an inmate family that is a member of your church, you as a volunteer *should not* be a go between with the inmate and his family in any way, including materially or by communication that may bypass the in-place policies of the institution, such as mail, money, legal help, or private messages from family no matter how innocent it seems. There are a myriad of security traps if you do.

Another confusing and sometimes unavoidable thing happens when someone you know is incarcerated and lands in an area where you are volunteering. You should let your institutional volunteer supervisor or chaplain know immediately. A wise supervisor will remove you from any means of interaction. That way, you won't be pressured by the family or the inmate to violate the rules by becoming an intermediary in anyway.

Now, let me address the church's choice to have a ministry to prisons by helping just the *families of inmates*. Family ministry of incarcerated inmates is road less traveled by the church. Usually, the focus is specifically just to families of inmates with no real direct contact with the inmate except perhaps through some program initiated from program managers inside the institution. But the key to this ministry is to ensure your program uses church volunteers distinctly focused on working with jail or prison staff who can be the go-between for information and referrals of those inmates to your program. Those volunteers should not have access to inmates from the inside. For instance, a person is a member of your church. The ministry has to have guidelines and clear goals and standards of measure for how that help translates. You never want to breed dependency or a continued cycle of behavior from the inmate and family. The goal should be to help people get on their feet so they can be independent, not dependent.

Growing up, I lived in several parsonages where the house was right by the church. We were often visited by people that made a living off of going from church to church with their sad stories. It was hard to tell which story was real and which weren't. But, after a while, they all had virtually the same script. A woman toting a toddler in hand would come to the door. A man in a beat-up car would sit in the car watching. The story line was they were just getting into town and the husband was starting work the following week and they needed help until then. These people had no intention of getting on their feet with the church's help. They were doing quite well just milking churches for "help." My point? Beware of inmates and their families who make a career of loafing and getting "help" from churches.

It's important to measure what helping really is. Be wise. Trust, but verify. Helping people who milk the church is taking away from those really in need of your help. It's okay to ask questions. Here are few questions that are good to ask. Having some information will help you know what *kind* of help, if any, to give.

In ministry to inmate families:

- Is your ministry just helping a family get on their feet because of the impact of the incarceration of their loved one? Or is your church ministry going to go whole hog and get involved with the incarcerated inmate as well? Again, it's complex, and my advice is to pick one. As volunteers, you can't be all things to all people even as a church. It will consume you.

- What steps has the head of the household taken to rectify their situation?
- Is the family in a codependent cycle? Are they hooked into the inmate's cycle of jail and release? Would your help simply continue that cycle? It pays to do your homework so that any help you give to inmate or family is wise use of the resources God has given your church.

Sometimes, the right answer to a request for help is *no.* At times, the only help you should give is making them aware of their cycle of enabling the incarcerated family member. It's helping them let go of help that always gives a soft emotional landing to their incarcerated member, while they take the brunt emotionally and financially of their decision.

In ministry to the inmate side that involves inside-out connection with community-based reentry, ask:

- How many times has this person been locked up?
- Do they have a drug problem?
- Has the inmate been in a community-based treatment program of any kind and relapsed?
- Does this person have a history of defective behavior with their family? For instance, has their family stopped helping them financially or any other way because of repetitive criminal behavior that is eating the life out of the family? Are they now trying to reconnect to their

family by getting your church involved trying to prove to the family a change of heart?

- What steps are they taking to help themselves?
- Are the above answers to questions verifiable?

You probably are aware by reading this chapter how complex the whole issue is. Pick the type of ministry angle you are called to, and stick to it. Compassion is a good thing, but that doesn't translate to being a pushover. Pray for wisdom in what help really is for each individual and what your level of involvement should be. Staying within that framework will do wonders at making your ministry effective.

CHAPTER 13

Advocating for Inmates

Within your ministry to inmates who are incarcerated, it's inevitable that spiritual mentoring relationships will develop. A level of trust will be achieved, and what they tell you can elicit empathy. Want to know how to derail your spiritual mission? Become an inmate advocate who takes up the complaints of an inmate who is claiming abuse by the system. Inmates may come to you claiming biased treatment and want you to take their story to their family, the administration, or even the press, thereby bypassing the chain of the pathways in place for those types of complaints by inmates.

Most of the time, you will be approached by inmates who want to get you between them and the system, but not for something egregious. One of the first things an inmate will ask prior to drawing you into their complaint is this: "Is this confidential?" Red flags should automatically go up. But the standard answer to that question is "Yes, unless it has to do with physical or sexual abuse of yourself or someone else or a potential escape." Then if the inmate continues and confides in you, it's one of two things: they want you to take the information to someone else, or they want you to put yourself between them and the consequences of some behavior issue they are being disciplined for.

The problem is this question may also be a precursor to a real issue as well. So, listen carefully to all that follows. By that, I mean you have to weigh the truth of the matter. Some inmates are really good at storytelling, trying to set you up for an "it's us against them" relationship that results in you being pulled into becoming their advocate against the system.

Be wise. Here are a few questions to ask initially after an inmate approaches you with a complaint:

- What institutional measures have you taken to deal with this?
- Have you told anyone else?
- Have you had a history of being disciplined?
- What is it you want me to do?

That way, you will get an idea where the inmate is coming from.

The biggest trap is in what an inmate *doesn't* tell you. Benjamin Franklin said, "Half a truth is often a great lie." And so it is with the majority of inmate complaints. Inmates will try to draw you into advocating for them against the system by telling you a half-truth. For instance, a claim of being restricted to quarters or not being allowed to write letters or make phone calls may be true, and it tugs at your heartstrings. After all, you may think, *They are already in jail or prison. Isn't additional punishment harsh?* It may seem so, but use your head. Is the inmate being sanctioned for a disciplinary reason? How does this institution maintain control over disruptive behavior? You have to know that bad behavior doesn't just stop when they are locked up. Prison is just a change of location for some, and their dysfunctional behavior doesn't just stop. Rules have to be in place as well as consequences when they are violated to maintain order in the institution.

Inmates can file grievances against the system in a myriad of ways internally from verbally complaining to the staff or warden or utilizing the internal grievance system and filing a written complaint, to filing a lawsuit through their outside attorney.

The majority of prisons and some larger jails hand out an inmate handbook that contains written rules when they are booked into the jail or prison. That handbook also gives the measure of punishment possible if they break the rules. If they violate a rule and are given a write-up by a staff member, they attend a type of institution court in front of a discipline-hearing officer, who determines guilt or innocence based on an internal investigation of the evidence contained in the write-up. Various punishments or "sanctions" are given if found guilty.

Jails are more limited in the selection of sanction methods, but their disruptive behavior may cause them to be moved to a segregated housing unit or cell or even charged with an additional crime depending on what occurred.

Prisons have more sanctions available, such as restriction to the unit, no phone calls, no letters, loss of visitation privileges, loss of good time, and other techniques intended to curb further bad behavior.

If, especially, egregious behavior has occurred, such as being found to be responsible for entry of drugs in to the facility or injury or death occurred in commission of any other violation, that inmate may be officially charged according to federal or state laws, and time may be added to their sentence.

For this discussion, in your spiritual mentor role, how should you address this type of complaint brought to you by the inmate? Simple. Don't get between the system and the discipline of an inmate. Hold your horses about going higher up. They may be throwing a tantrum about sanctions they deserved.

Let me make a clarification before I end this chapter. Clearly, I'm not talking about claims of sexual abuse or physical mistreatment by other inmates or even a staff member. If an inmate comes to you with those types of issues, you *must* take it to a higher up *before* you leave the institution. Something is happening, and they trust no one in the system. Bringing you into it is a desperate move for them. They may be afraid to go to a staff member at their level of interaction and can't get to a higher up with fear of retaliation or their issue is inmate related and they fear being labeled a snitch by their peers. In prison, that's almost a death sentence. If it is about a staff member, they may be afraid the system won't protect them. When a volunteer comes into the mix, they may see you as a person that can get the message to the right people. Most of the time, they will verbally tell you. Other times, they will slip you a note. Again, *do not* leave the institution without making that report. A life may be on the line.

As a chaplain, I've had many inmates come to me who were being abused in some way. In prisons, visiting with a chaplain usually isn't seen as suspect by other inmates or staff. I was able to get the message to the right people in the institution. So if there's a chaplain, that's your first stop. The chaplain is the best bet, but if there is no chaplain, whoever is out of the realm of line staff, such as a lieutenant captain, jail administrator, associate warden, or even the prison warden, is an option.

You may be asking, Won't the inmate be in danger if a staff member is involved somehow? Won't it be slow timed or even put the inmate in jeopardy? There are no easy answers especially in hypothetical examples, but here's an interesting dynamic. Once a free world volunteer has knowledge of a threat to an inmate, it puts a type of hands-off barrier to certain types of retaliation. You know about it. The system has to address it because, in the end, you have the power to take it outside the system and make it public.

Caution: remember that, here, we are talking about something egregious, not a simple grievance over a disciplinary problem. Never use that power frivolously, or you doom your ability to volunteer. My point is weigh the information, and take your best intelligent shot at getting it to the right person, starting with inside staff. Ask questions initially of the inmate complaining to you, but after the initial conversation with the inmate, ask those questions to those people who can check out the inmate's story officially. Take it to the chaplain or official if you deem the inmate has come to you with something that can't be ignored. But guard your credibility. Don't be the investigator.

How can you make the most of a complaint by an inmate whose complaints don't rise to an egregious level? Take the opportunity to teach spiritual principles in the moment to the inmate. Actions have consequences. How could they have handled their situation better? Help them with better communication and behavior skills coupled with scriptural foundations. That can equip them for better responses to whatever situation they encounter. That's where your responsibility ends. You can't fix things for them. Remember:

you cannot be a buffer to their emotions or deliver them from the consequences of actions, but you can be a listener and pray with them. You can also be their teacher and equip them with better behavior skills based on what Jesus would do.

CHAPTER 14

Volunteers and Competition between Religious Groups

Speaking as a Christian, I know what my mission is. That mission is to share the gospel of Jesus Christ. Scripture says there is no other way to God except though Christ. As Christians, we have a commission to take that truth everywhere. But how that's served up matters. My beliefs don't translate to engaging in a crusade to talk down another belief. My mission is to relate to others like Jesus did. Jesus didn't waver in what he presented, but he did meet people where they were in their life, engaging in fruitful conversation that allowed for the sharing of the good news. He loved and engaged people. He didn't coerce them.

Remember what this book is about. I'm trying to help you be "streetwise" in a secular world that for your mission is refined to a jail or prison ministry. You are entering a small capsule of the world when you minster in jails and prisons. That means you are going to run into fellow volunteers and inmates from other denominations that do not hold to your application of the scripture or, for that matter, even Christianity. It's important to respect the group who may be coming in at the same time for a program or that inmate who may present a doctrine with which you may not agree.

That doesn't mean holding back on discussion with that person. It's totally fine to engage in consensual conversation and ask questions of others and let them ask you questions regarding your faith, so you can, as scripture says, give an answer why you believe. If a situation presents itself and a discussion ensues with a person not of your faith, by all means, engage in conversation, but not debate. Religious discussion can get passionate, can't it? Don't put the chaplain in the middle of that where the division necessitates an intervention. And certainly do not have those debates in front of inmates. I've known some pretty obnoxious volunteers and even preachers that turn on the chaplain when the chaplain has to run interference between groups. There's certainly no excuse for having debates with another group or bad-mouthing them to inmates on the fine points of the Christian faith.

That advice, of course, crosses to discussions with volunteers and inmates of non-Christian faiths. Remember: prisons are a cross-cultural sample of the United States and even at times foreign countries. The non-Christian groups may include various sects of Judaism, Islam, Sikhs, American Indian, Rastafarian, Buddhism, Asatru, Odinism, Wicca, Satanism, and, well, you get the idea. That list doesn't even include religions *created* by people who merge parts of various religions and make up their own beliefs. And don't forget the agnostics and atheist that have the self-appointed mission of challenging people of faith of all religions and claim the same rights as religious groups to spread their antireligious message, all but making themselves a religion.

Very interesting conversations can be had with people of other faiths. I've had numerous conversations with many people and have been able to share the gospel uninhibited because of that interchange in discussion of the differences in beliefs. Sharing the gospel is just part of that conversation, and truth always rises to the top. Calm assurance of your beliefs in such an exchange may plant a seed. You don't have to have a neutered discussion with other faith groups, but I reiterate: don't cross the line to debate and start kicking up dust on each other.

You should set an example of how to have that kind of conversation especially in front of inmates. That kind of debate between volunteers can trickle down to inmates who also hold to that doctrine. They can mess with your ministry big time, even to try to interrupt your services as well as start a religious war between inmates in the institution. Some can get pretty rude, and many volunteers don't know quite how to handle an inmate of another religion, challenging them to the point of disruption and taking over. The best way is to let the chaplain handle it, but if you are forced into that situation, deal with it graciously but with firmness.

Some non-Christian faith groups encourage their followers to attend Christian programming, but not for positive reasons. They have an agenda to coerce others to leave their Christian faith for what they claim are their true religious roots found in African or Middle Eastern countries. They even try this in the free world. Free world preachers have had to get aggressive and order them to leave. But, in prison, it's a potentially volatile issue on a different level. In prison, this behavior may continue. Disrespecting another's faith can flame literal holy wars inmates may act on.

I was monitoring a volunteer lead service once. This was a preaching service, not a question-and-answer bible study. The preacher had just started preaching, and an inmate right on the front row began to interrupt him by asking comparative religious questions. The volunteer was trying to get a handle on what to do. Ordinarily, only in bible study formats are questions appropriate. I, however, recognized what religion the inmate was and what his intentions were. I intervened, saying, "Sir, while you are certainly welcome to attend any religious service, you are not allowed to disrupt. You knew what religion this service was when you came. Now, you can sit and listen, or you are welcome to leave right now." He chose to stay, obviously not happy or expecting anyone to challenge his behavior.

Another time, several of this same non-Christian group attended the main Protestant service. I was filling in for another chaplain at that institution. I was going over my notes while an inmate led a testimony time. One member of that group stood and identified himself as that denomination and began to expound on their doctrine. He finished and sat down. Immediately, another inmate stood and began to expound again on their religious doctrine. It dawned on me what was happening. I did not let him finish. I went to the podium and interrupted his speech by thanking him for coming and told them they were welcome but not to interject their doctrine using this forum. I reminded him this was a Christian service and told him to sit down.

When the song service began, a note was passed to me from an inmate in the congregation. It said, "Chaplain, that must have been hard, but thank you so much for stopping them from taking over our service."

I called those inmates to my office later and told them I knew what they were doing and not to let it happen again or I'd write them up. They both denied my accusation, so I did write them up for disruptive behavior that could have caused some type of holy war between the groups. They had done a major disrespectful intrusion into another groups worship service.

This competitive behavior happens from time to time, and you have to take charge. If you can't find a way to shut down the behavior, let the chaplain know.

Less-calculated behavior may occur out of the blue. Inmates will attend most any chapel service where they may hear you preach a doctrine contrary to what they were just taught by a volunteer group that may have preceded you or what they have been taught from their own faith from their youth. They may be particularly aggressive because you are rattling their foundation. Many inmates have gotten back into their familiar denominational family while incarcerated and will try to hold the fort if you teach something contrary to what they grew up with. You may have just challenged their last familiar foundation. They are barely keeping their head above water as it is, so friction will occur. When this occurs, respect the challenge and pray about how to answer without turning it into a debate.

I challenge you to review how Jesus responded to those who were in error doctrinally and tried to pick fights verbally with him in both passive and aggressive manners. And that includes being wise enough to recognize when *not* to even engage in a discussion with someone, inmate or volunteer. Jesus used the adage not to cast pearls before swine. Just don't be that person who has to turn a friendly discussion into a word battle to come out on top of the debate that forces the chaplain to have to become an arbitrator.

CHAPTER 15

The Gender Issue in Jail and Prison Ministry

It's a topic as old as the first man and woman—that old friction that sometimes deteriorates into the battle between the sexes. In spiritual life, that shouldn't happen but often does. God created two genders complete with so-called weaknesses and strengths that complement each other. It's obvious throughout scripture there is no doctrine of competition or subjugation by genders that is intended by God. Both fulfill their purpose in the kingdom of God. God's love and plan for us in relationship with Him are not gender based. It is only in the application of traditions and interpretation of roles that competition and tension begin. Unintentionally in not only religious circles but also the secular world, gender tension is in play in everyday life, in our workplace, in our recreational life, and in unexpected situations. And, to the point, you will encounter those natural issues of gender in ministry. Don't pretend you are immune to those. I'm going to spend a long time on this subject. Please pay attention. It has many tentacles, so you'll find this chapter will chase a few rabbits.

First, just a pointer that will keep your integrity from being compromised. Never hang back after a chapel service to counsel alone. This applies to both genders especially in this day and age where same-sex attraction is a possibility. It's common in open chapel church services for inmates to linger to talk one on one with volunteers. That's fine as long as everyone else is in the area. If you find yourself alone with an inmate who wants to talk, get yourself moving to a less isolating area. You have legs. Use them. Joseph *ran* from Potiphar's wife. There's no shame in that. The principle is the same here. If the inmate is above board, they won't have a problem with you taking charge of time and location for your moment of personal counseling. Always have a chaplain or another volunteer in the vicinity if the conversation is going to go beyond just casual chatting while waiting to leave the institution. There should always at least be others in the area visibly.

Even full-time chaplains have rules they go by when doing personal counseling. My practice, even as a departmental chaplain, was to alert a lieutenant when I had to call an inmate from the unit to give emergency messages when the chapel was not active. Rumors can start really fast by inmates and staff when someone is getting personal attention, even when necessary. During regular chapel hours, because my office had large windows, inmates assigned to work in the chapel were usually in full view. I had an open-door policy for counseling but listened carefully and could tell when an inmate was just seeking company, not help with their problems.

Let me add here that sometimes we are just not in tune with an inmate using us to gratify himself. Realistically, you can't catch everything. So, don't be insulted or defensive if another volunteer or even an inmate warns you about how another inmate is interacting with you. Interestingly, inmates often have your back, though you never want to be party officially to the habit of allowing inmates to run interference for you. That may be a trap in itself. But many inmates will watch over you from a distance when known sexual predators are circling. Several times, my inmate office trustees informed me after the fact of the intentions of various inmates vying for attention or making certain gestures around me. I always listened and weighed why they were telling me but never tossed their warnings away.

Let's get technical on opposite gender ministry now. Regardless of your feelings on women and men in various roles, it does impact volunteer ministry in jails and prisons. The spotlight on gender is much more under scrutiny in jail ministry than prison ministry. Depending on the structure of the jail, ministry is usually right outside the unit separated by bars and is limited to same-sex ministry for a myriad of security reasons. But you never know. One large-capacity high-rise jail was actually locking the volunteers inside the jail unit TV room. I never could understand the sanity behind that even for same-sex ministry.

Prison ministry most often takes place in a room or chapel, not in the units. Churches send small groups that include both male and female and provide a congregate program including bible series with applicable daily life application, short bible studies, or a worship service. Either way, gender is always a factor to consider when forming jail and prison teams. Make sure your team members are mature Christians and not emotionally needy.

I'm a firm believer in accountability in ministry, so, first, it's imperative to bring your particular church leadership into the mix before even starting your ministry inside. Some denominations interpret the scriptures in a way that narrowly defines gender roles in sharing of the gospel even in their church, much less as a volunteer missionary in a jail or prison. One pastor will prohibit women from ministering to men, while other pastors in that same denomination have no issue with it. Paradoxically, that same denomination won't have an issue with a male ministering in a jail or prison to women in spite of the obvious traps possible there. It can be confusing even for members of those denominations. But your chosen church has a say in how they want you to function. You can maintain your calling without bucking your own church guidelines, though that may be hard to navigate. I say that because most jails and prisons will want you to be connected with a church rather than flying solo without a denominational connection. The issue of opposite gender jail and prison ministry starts there.

Even if your denomination has no issue with opposite gender ministry, they aren't the final word. However you land on the role of gender in ministry, you are coming into a place where many aberrant behaviors are condensed. And whatever higher application of opposite gender ministry you wish to apply, in ministry, you have to face the fact you will run into not only sexual tensions but gender biases regarding roles from correctional staff, chaplains, other volunteers, and even inmates. A correctional facility sets those perimeters depending on the size of the place, access setup, and type of programming. Some administrations won't support opposite gender volunteers especially in jails, and some restrict it in certain levels of prison security because of staffing issues or perceptions of the personal security risks to civilians.

I'll be up front with you on why I'm being so blunt. Some people choose to bring their personal crusades to their ministry. Don't do that. Forcing the issue for some personal power issue isn't productive. Remember: it's not about you but about sharing the gospel. Integrity takes time to establish, and you'll find you'll be less restricted in movement in the jail once you are established and stay fixed on why you are there. That statement is for both male and female volunteers. You'll be surprised what doors open for you regardless of gender when God opens it instead of you pushing through doors closed to you.

Is cross-gender ministry in jail and prisons ever workable? Speaking as a female chaplain who ministered to male inmates for the larger part of my thirty-one years as a full-time jail and prison chaplain, the answer to that question is obvious. Yes, for some, it's possible. But the caveat is I wasn't a volunteer. I was paid professional staff endorsed by my denomination as both a chaplain and missionary, and while I did apply to various same-sex prisons during my career, I was selected for all-male prisons by the interviewers that determined my course. I never pursued it as a crusade. Time and again, I was selected for all-male institutions. I never really thought about it as proving anything. I just fit there. Sometimes, God puts you where people think you should not be. When I ran into those biases mentioned, though, believe it or not, those were few and far between, I'd listen but didn't get sidetracked with being pulled into religious debates on the subject. My mission was to be the presence of God in ministry where He planted me. I went through doors opening for me. I never pushed through. I let anyone objecting take it up with God and continued doing what God had me doing.

In my denomination prior to endorsement to chaplaincy missions, there is a required interview by a psychologist. He suddenly fixed eyes on me and asked, "How'd you get so strong?" His question surprised me. I don't remember my answer, but I do remember the question. And still the question baffles me. People with callings may question their *application* of ministry at times, but never their calling. It's just natural. *They just know,* and they are content to follow that path step by step without so-called permission to do so or listening to the naysayers telling them they can't. They don't waste time defending their calling but simply walk in the direction of that calling, trusting God to open and close doors. It's not a crusade, just a faith walk totally dependent on God.

What makes one "strong"? It's total dependency on God alone. I followed the course God set for *me.* My whole twenty-year career with the feds was in male prisons. After all, God chooses who He wants to place in such roles. My path was not a model for others, just my path as God directed me. The entire Bible attests to the fact that God's ways are not our ways. God's big picture defies denominational interpretation of roles from time to time.

My perspective in working in men's prisons was sharing the gospel and growing disciples. That's not a gender issue. It's the same thing like-minded men in specialized ministry focus on. Gender may bring different application and technique because women and men think and organize differently, but it doesn't change the message. The truth of the message of Christ doesn't change because of the gender speaking it. There is neither male nor female in Christ. The gospel is the gospel. We all have that missions calling.

How did the majority of staff and inmates respond to me? With staff, much like biblical Deborah. She gave counsel to the captains of armies and was judge over matters for the Israelite people. They trusted her with leadership and respected her counsel. And inmates? I once had an inmate wish me a happy Mother's Day. I said, "Well, thank you, but I'm not a mother." He looked at me with respect and said. "Yes, you are. You are the mother of the church." That confirmed how I had always generally thought. These men needed something the male gender can't teach them in application. They needed a godly female role model who was virtuous and dedicated to the Lord and to learn how to respect a woman as a godly man would. A mother nurtures and teaches. She corrects her children because she loves them, and sometimes harshly. She teaches her son to love God, his wife, and his family. She teaches him responsibility as a man from a woman's perspective to provide and protect. So, yes, there is a place for women in cross-gender ministry. And, yes, it's biblical.

Having shared a small bit of my personal path, you can assume I learned a lot about cross-gender ministry, both good and bad, in those twenty years of working in the federal system. Opposite gender ministry is certainly not that simple. You'd do well to scout it out thoroughly before announcing that's for you. And, remember: I'm addressing men as well. Don't be naïve. The influence of biological and emotional differences especially in a place as dysfunctional as a jail or prison is just a fact of life. And, as stated, same-sex ministry is probably best for most volunteers unless it's a mixed team going into prisons for programming, and even then, there are precautions that always have to be taken.

Those disagreeing with this opinion argue that their faith in God can break down any roadblock to their ability to minister to the opposite gender. Stop with the religiosity, and have some common sense. It's your business as a child of a God called to specific ministry to know all the angles of your calling. So, as a starting point, lay aside the piety, and let's weigh whether you are one of the few who can minister effectively to the opposite sex in jails and prisons.

You have to remember the inmate is already in a highly vulnerable state emotionally. Transference of feelings to a person who suddenly comes into your life in an emotionally trying time is not unusual. The inmate can easily apply wrong interpretations of attention to that volunteer who shares peace, empathizes with their situation, and gives a listening ear. That attentive dedicated inmate who doesn't ever miss your service just may have a crush on you. And possibly you are in danger of having a crush as well if you don't watch yourself emotionally.

It's always a good idea to do a spiritual and emotional self-check each time you go into the prison or jail. Where are *you* emotionally that day? Feeling lonely? Put upon? Unappreciated? We all do at times, but you can't afford to be out of touch with these feelings when entering the prison. Retired, divorced, never married, and people who are experiencing lulls of gratification in their married or work lives are vulnerable to their own misfire of emotions when an inmate pours it on with gratitude, attention, and a need to please you as though you are the center of their world. So, slap yourself out of it when you go into the prison, and make sure you are spiritually task oriented each time you go in. You need it to be about Him all the time anyway regardless of what gender you minister to.

People relate to war stories, so I'm going to use a few to illustrate mistakes both genders have made. If something strikes a chord with you in any of these stories, ask yourself why.

WOMEN TO MEN

A very proficient and godly woman volunteered in a county jail and had the respect of the staff there to the point where she was put on the payroll coordinating the religious programming for that facility. She conducted herself well for years and kept to the spiritual boundaries. Then there was that one inmate. He was sick. She spent extra time with him for studies. Conversations started to get personal, but she rationalized them to be in the spiritual realm of personal. Her thinking was that a good Christian should relate to people in prison as a brother or sister in Christ. She thought Christ was the great equalizer. This is what I call the trap of "taking your professional hat off." Her thinking went to the utopian idea that what he was in prison for was not important. Her rationalization evolved. Who knows, she thought, but that God might have brought them together for such a time as this. This was the naïve, wrong thinking that dumbed down her common sense and allowed her to talk herself into a romantic notion regarding the inmate.

He was transferred from the county jail to a federal medical facility, where his illness advanced and he was diagnosed as terminal. They had continued corresponding when he had been transferred. He had lately begun to ask her to come visit him. She tried using her clergy label for a visit and was denied.

Commonly, her credentials and past association in another facility would be enough to get her in. But federal and state laws often conflict, and they did not want to honor her request to have a clergy visit. She contacted me, asking me for help to visit this man.

I asked for more information. It's not uncommon for chaplains to respond to letters received by those who were impacted by their ministry after they get out or are sent to other facilities. At times, a letter of encouragement is proper and rarely even a visit, but something in the tone of the intensity of her plea for me to help her get access to the prison waved the red flags for me. She laid it out to me in a rather lengthy letter. It didn't take long for me to understand why she was red-flagged by prison personnel, since inmate correspondence received and sent is monitored. Their blooming affection was spoken of in the letters he sent to her, always couched in the most proper spiritual terms, but she was trying to enter using her role as chaplain. She had continued to rationalize a spiritual motive for wanting to see him and even excused half-truths. She was blind to the problem because she was emotionally involved. Her reasoning was that no one could determine the ways of God in how He brought people together, and, besides, this man was dying and he needed her. She pled with me to validate her to the staff at the prison so they would know she was above board in intentions. She thought that with my being a woman and with my experience working in men's prisons, somehow, I'd be her strongest advocate and I could influence the administration to allow her to see the man in her capacity as a jail chaplain.

I told her candidly she had forgotten her mission and that mistake was about to cause her to sacrifice her ministry. God had put her in a high-profile position to impact inmates for His purpose and glory. If she fell to a personal relationship with one of her spiritual clients, she was jeopardizing not only her integrity with the staff but also the God-given oversight of inmates and volunteers. My advice to her was to immediately withdraw any contact with the inmate in any way. No letters. No going through anyone to him. No nothing. Turn him over to God. Her rescue mentality was hindering what God was doing in this inmates' life and was keeping him from depending on God alone. She had made herself as the substitute, and the inmate turned his focus from God to her. I encouraged her to speak with her pastor and the jail administrator where she worked. Based on those conversations, she was to determine whether she should continue to minister in her capacity.

Here are a few principle rules I followed when working with the opposite gender in jails and prisons. First, I decided my work in that person's life was done when an inmate transferred to another facility. But if some odd request were to come from a past inmate, I determined to go through the chaplain at their new site *for accountability.*

Another mode of operation I used was if the inmate was released and I received correspondence, I had another staff initial the letter or bring them in on the content if only in casual dialog *for accountability.* If a phone call was received at work, I took the time to talk, but, afterward, I did not initiate other calls unless it was informational regarding a request they had made for resources in the free world. I did not continue to counsel them over the phone. I tried to connect them up with local pastors and other volunteer agencies that specialize in *released* inmates.

MEN TO WOMEN

Men are no less susceptible to emotional transference and getting off track when they deal with female inmates. Sad to say, I personally knew a male chaplain of my own denomination who set aside his mission and compromised some of his female charges and ultimately spent time in prison. And, regretfully, he is not an exception. I recently read of another prison chaplain who got involved with a female inmate. This professional chaplain who had all the training spiritually and secularly to all the traps fell hard and shattered the faith of many already fragile women, not to mention the violation of the trust of staff by fracturing their perspective of religious practices in prison. He also did prison time.

This is a good place to point out the double standard that often traps men into a false sense of security in ministry to the opposite sex. In some denominational circles, they deny women the ability to minister to men while condoning men to minister to women in the same capacity. If professional male chaplains can be compromised, what makes you think male religious volunteers are not as susceptible when working with female inmates? So, men, do not think you have some magical protection around you when ministering in prisons to the opposite sex.

Paradoxically, while men should function with the same information I just gave to women ministering to men, the dynamics are slightly different. Men do have emotions too but apply them differently. Women ordinarily respond to the pain in men *with nurturing, advice, and direction*. Men respond to women in pain *with protection, advice, and direction*.

Men in ministry to women have to deal with women who are seeking male attention with a confused emotional system that many times has them defining love by sexual encounters. They simply do not know how to respond or interpret a godly teacher that is a man giving them attention. Men have to be especially accountable to others when dealing with incarcerated women. Sexual attraction is built into us and can easily go off the rails in a correctional setting if not put in perspective and under the control of the Lord. The most spiritual man just living his godly character in his ministry can be misinterpreted by a female inmate as a signaling of interest in her outside his spiritual mission, and, all of a sudden, she concludes love is in the air.

Why does that trap exhibit itself more in jail and prison ministry? Incarcerated women usually have not had good male role models. And if a father or good male role model is absent or has been neglectful or abusive, it leaves a hole in her life. A father is very important in the life of a female child. He teaches her strength from a man's perspective. He gives her information on how men think and what they want. He teaches her respect for her body. He protects her against men who would try to manipulate love into mere sexual gratification. He protects her while she grows up and explores life and allows her to try her wings in ways a mom would never do. He's there to comfort if she gets disappointed or hurt, not so much in words but in presence and just the strong arm of comfort with no strings attached.

In a correctional setting, women may purposely try to wile the affections of a man. The lure of women is always there for a man, and it can turn inappropriate in a wink. Remember what Joseph went through? It can happen to you. I guarantee you it only takes one woman to make even the slightest accusation of impropriety for a man of God to lose his reputation. So, think really hard if you are thinking you as a man are called to minister in women's jails and prisons as an individual or on a team. Even free world pastors have fallen into wolf traps.

I'll give you two examples. A man was ministering to a woman on death row. His intentions were good at the time, and he was faithful to come in and do bible studies. Then she got her execution date. The emotions spiraled as appeals for stays were on the table constantly. He was her spiritual advisor and was allowed to continue the one-on-one studies with her, though only conveyed through a glass window. Then he forgot his mission, and his protection mode went into overdrive. He began to interpret these feelings as love. She returned his feelings. He reasoned he was there for her for such a time as this. She was going to die. She deserved someone who loved her with a godly love. They'd never be able to consummate the love, so it was to them a glorified spiritual love. There was a proposal and a marriage. And, yes, marriages can be permitted in prisons.

What went wrong here? Was the thinking along the lines of who can say whether their love was all in God's plan for her final moments prior to her execution? To me, that's a pretty shallow view of eternity. She is about to die and go into the arms of the Lord—for a Christian, the ultimate transition—and all he is thinking is her temporal happiness? His mission in coming into a prison was not to search and find a wife. It was to disciple her and to help her grow spiritually regardless of how long she had yet to live on this earth. Her witness to those around her, though she was facing death, was powerful. Wouldn't you, if you were Satan, want to divert the subject from the eternal to the temporal and to keep her from blessing those around her through her faith? But in her last hours, it was all for the volunteer.

I'm not so coldhearted at someone's last moments that I think they should face it alone. This woman faced death unafraid, and her testimony was gallant. But, pragmatically, the intense one-on-one ministry between this male minister and the female inmate was an accident waiting to happen, especially dealing with life-and-death issues. I can't imagine he didn't see the red flags at some point when experiencing feelings for the female inmate. He should have listened and handed off ministry with her to a same-sex volunteer. However, this male volunteer, in forgetting his mission, sacrificed any further credibility to minister in jails and prisons.

I'll give a second illustration for men. This involves a professional male chaplain in a large county jail. Time and again, I candidly told him that putting an arm around female inmates even when she was grieving at bad news was not necessary, and certainly not keeping his door open when counseling a female was asking for trouble.

A couple of years after I had left for another chaplaincy position, I learned he had been accused by a female inmate of sexual advances. I didn't believe it for a minute. He was a kind and dedicated chaplain. He simply had disregarded my warning and walked into an old trap women often use. She wanted a payout from the county knowing most counties avoid the publicity, choosing to settle out of court. But this county didn't. He was suspended while an investigation was held. No evidence was found that could validate the inmate's claims. No other women came forward. No formal charges were brought.

That should have vindicated him. But the inmate actually sued him in civil court. Again, he was found innocent, but there was no way he was going to personally minister in jails ever again. A man even accused is seen as guilty. His ministry credibility was over. I just shook my head when I heard. Why hadn't he listened to me? Truly, pride goes before a fall.

Here's a spiritual tip. God always sends you warnings, sometimes in the strangest ways. Although people have various motives for giving you unsolicited advice or observations, always listen graciously with spiritual ears no matter how much experience you've had in jail or prison ministry. Weigh what they are saying. Pray about it. They may just be the whisper of God to keep you out of trouble.

SAME-SEX ATTRACTION

I'll speak to one more thing regarding gender in jail and prison ministry. Front and center in our day is the issue of *same-sex attraction*. Don't think for a minute just because you deal with the same gender, you won't encounter an inmate who is attracted to you romantically. Gender dysphoria is real for some people and wrestle daily with those feelings of attraction to the same sex. And on the other side of that, many just choose to embrace sexual attractions that may run toward same-sex choices. Ninety-five percent of the time, these individuals define everything by their sexuality. Again, there is the condensed emotional factor you are dealing with in jails and prisons that can enhance their lack of good judgment and self-control. So, get prepared. The same lessons already mentioned apply to these gender-confused people as well.

Their overtures may be a bit more subtle, however. But go with your gut.

A person with same-sex attraction may be drawn to you as a volunteer at first because of your confidence in your faith. Your strength of knowledge in God's word gives them hope they can find relief from their struggle and inner conflict about why they are attracted to same sex. They see you as someone with answers, and they desperately want answers as to why they feel different. They want to feel accepted and normal.

The people I have known who struggle with same-sex attractions have sought the solace and safety of same-sex attraction because it's less stressful. From a woman's point of view, another woman comprehends the depth of their emotional struggle in a way a man wouldn't. And, in turn, a man receiving validation from another man makes him feel less odd. He's found a kindred spirit. It's more complicated than that, of course. People who struggle with or even embrace the homosexual lifestyle frame everything by sexuality and feelings rather than biology or spiritual laws.

If they are a new believer who is struggling with those feelings, it's importation to emphasis that our relationship with Christ is *validated on the fact of God's promises, not a feeling about them.* You teach them that principle. But it is a struggle. And they will always look to create their own truth by justifying their choices as okay and reason there's nothing wrong with loving someone.

Society reinforces the myth that embracing same-sex attraction is as normal as the standard set by God in opposite gender attraction. They'll even blend scriptural principles into their argument. God understands their struggle but still requires conformity to his standards. It's like any other addiction with the excuses and constant craving for validation of self. However, this struggle is about more than addiction or obsession. Even subconsciously, it's a core struggle that God somehow made a mistake and they are in the wrong body.

As a volunteer, you are not there to counsel such a long-term struggle, though some may try to engage you that way. The endgame is to help them learn to depend on God alone. Help them to stop focusing on their struggle but on the facts and principles of the Word. God will do the rest.

For this discussion, just be aware of the possibility a same-sex-attracted person may hit on you as quickly as someone not in that struggle. Deal with it the same way you would any other sexual overture. If you become uncomfortable, go with your gut. You don't have to be right about it, nor do you have to investigate it or ignore it. Engage your volunteer supervisor, whether chaplain or volunteer coordinator. Bringing in a third person for perspective and problem solving is perfectly in order. By bringing in those who are over your ministry, you may discover you weren't the first person that inmate had tried to compromise. You will also gain some knowledge in how to deal with these types of advances in the future.

Don't be so prideful as to think you can take care of it yourself. It won't go away no matter how minor much less egregious. Silence gives power to the situation. Rejection can spur false accusations from an inmate. Believe me, it keeps you safe if the inmate knows you are involving a third party. It does wonders to solve the problem. These accountability rules are imperative for a volunteer. If you sense an attraction beginning, do not attempt to speak to the inmate alone or by letter. Speak to the chaplain or program coordinator.

Accountability for both genders is imperative when working in jail and prison ministry. Look. Everyone in ministry can get distracted from time to time. That doesn't mean you are incompetent. When our inner warning signals are short-circuiting, it's best to take heed if something doesn't feel right and you have to talk yourself into justifying your choices. If someone warns you a train is coming, just get off the track and pray about it until you get a better perspective, that's all. That's why no matter how competent and familiar with your ministry you are, make sure you have someone you trust to give you counsel. Truth hurts sometimes, but it can save your ministry. It is a perversion of that ministry when romantic personal entanglements divert the focus from their spiritual journey.

And, by the way, as a side note, as a jail volunteer, if the inmate keeps making overtures, in most cases, the inmate will *not* be transferred or moved to another floor where you don't minster. You are in someone else's house, and the institution most often will not be moving inmates around for a volunteer. You'll be the one who needs to go. Just consider that God's intervention. In a prison, they can't be prohibited from chapel services unless they do something egregious and documentable. Again, *you* may have to stop coming into *that* prison.

CHAPTER 16

The Subtle Dangers of Touch in Prison Ministry

The last chapter on gender issues begs for this chapter on touching. I was watching a video of a well-known prison ministry whose programs are very grounded. I rejoice in their dedication and obvious training. But as I watched this video, I cringed when I watched a female volunteer reach out and touch the shoulder of a praying male inmate. People. It's best to keep your hands to yourself when volunteering in jails and prisons. And that includes you men as well. That may sound extreme, but remember: this is not your church. It's a prison, and the dynamics are different. But let me go on to expound on this for you before your head explodes.

Human beings need touch. A firm handshake, a friendly slap on the back, or a good hug can rejuvenate the spirit in a way no words can. Inmates are starved for touch. While handshakes and hugs may seem harmless and acceptable in your church, affection starved inmates can abuse it. I recommend as the standard the plumb line of no hugs and limited handshakes, even with your own gender and certainly never for the opposite gender in jail and prison ministry.

Let me work through a few things with you and start with handshakes. While a handshake is basically benign, remember: it may be just a handshake to you, but to the other person, it may mean physical contact with a not-so-innocent emotional meaning. Yes, that brief handshake is usually benign. But while that lingering handshake in the setting of your church is a gracious intent on connection, in a jail or prison environment, the inmate may be telegraphing a blooming unhealthy emotional or romantic attachment.

Here's another thing to consider. There's a physical security angle as well. Rarely do you see correctional staff shake an inmate's hand. It's been done, but not as a rule. An inmate can hang on to your hand and draw you in, putting you off balance and in harm's way for a sucker punch or even sexual gratification.

Hugs. A nice hug at the right moment is a message of encouragement without words, isn't it? But use your words, not physical touch, to encourage when doing ministry in jails and prisons. It's very rare a hug is imperative in jail and prison ministry.

The best-case scenario is for the chaplain or whoever the administration is to already have set the guidelines for inmates and physical contact prior to you even coming in. But sometimes nothing works, and it just happens you find yourself being pulled into a hug. Paradoxically, there are times a handshake can be a useful *preventative* tool if you are reading the body language that a hug is coming. When you read the signs, just stick out your hand and do a stiff handshake and don't allow them to draw you in even to one of those slight hugs. In jails and prisons, sometimes nothing works with the touchy-feely person, and you just have to speak out. It can get awkward, but find a way, perhaps saying something like, "I don't do any hugs or handshakes in here. I'm sure you understand." If that's too hard for you, elaborate and blame it on the rules. "I'm sorry. I know this is awkward, but it's nothing personal, and I'm sure you'll understand, but we aren't allowed to shake hands or hug."

What about the accidental touch? Those accidental touching incidents are not uncommon when large group programing is happening. Beware of the inmate initiated "accidental" touch. Listen. I'm not calling for paranoia here. Just use your common sense. There are often inmates milling around after programs who brush against you. These accidental brushes against you are quite often *not* accidental. When these touches happen, we prefer to ignore it, right? Reality check: ignoring it won't make it go away if it was intentional. You can confront it personally by acknowledging the "accidental" touch by a simple "excuse me" and moving away. But pay attention when that inmate is around if you have suspicions. You don't need to handle it yourself entirely. Bring the chaplain or program coordinator into the issue even when you are pretty sure it was an accident. They can monitor groups and remind the inmates of guidelines regarding proper spacing behavior with guest when you won't be implicated.

Most often, an inmate engaging in the so-called accidental touching is putting out feelers as to your street savvy and your embarrassment quotient. You may be being groomed for some potential compromise. You are seen as a sheep among wolves. Reframe that for them. Present yourself as a sheepdog. Be wise. On these issues, be straight up with the inmate. Don't worry about pushing them away spiritually. Coddling dysfunctional behavior only makes you look weak to them. They will not respect what you bring spiritually if they think you are an easily manipulated mark. Besides, you are there to give them the word, not protect their feelings.

There are so many variables for you to think about. Touching can actually be dangerous in a prison environment. Spiritual people are used to just giving a comforting touch, nothing lingering, just a touch of encouragement, maybe a pat on the back maybe after counseling session or particularly uplifting worship service. Be careful. You might just get decked. There are some inmates with mental problems and are very threatened by any touch. And some inmates see a touch as making them appear weak if done in front of other inmates. Other considerations include various religions that have rules against touching from opposite genders or even a religion other than their own.

In my early years as a chaplain, I learned the hard way about that. Thank God for our chapel officer. I had been counseling with a grief-stricken inmate earlier, and as he was leaving the chapel on the move with other inmates, I simply gave his shoulder a pat of encouragement. The chapel officer stopped him from decking me. No reason was given for that completely off-the-wall response. Maybe he was angry at being locked up when a relative died. Maybe he thought it was another inmate touching him. Maybe it just made him look weak to the other inmates. Who knows?

Another time, I was doing rounds in the dining hall and simply walked by a man who had made eye contact with me and gave him a pat on the shoulder. He growled, "Get your hands off me." He didn't have to tell me twice, and I just kept walking. But I learned. Use your words to comfort. Don't rely on touches.

Brace yourself for the next few comments. They are graphic. Sexually depraved inmates are proficient at getting their gratification and really don't care why you are there. Don't expect that everyone will respect your mission. Self-touching does occur. Sometimes, an inmate will come to the service inappropriately dressed, buttons unbuttoned or, in contrast, a too tight uniform. Male inmates sometimes leave their crotch flap open purposefully to flash you or more easily fondle themselves in services. In women's prisons, females will leave top buttons undone or shorten their clothing. Don't ignore this. Let the chaplain or officer know. They should remove that inmate from your program.

If you work in a jail and prison long enough, you will subjected to some very shocking sexual things during your volunteer time. I was holding services in a large prison chapel once and had an inmate sitting on the second row actually pull out his privates and fondle himself. I suppose he thought I'd never call him out in front of everyone. He was wrong. My embarrassment quotient was dulled down a long time ago. I stopped mid sentence and pointed to him and ordered him out of the room without explanation. He exited the main chapel for the chapel lobby. I continued the service. I later wrote an incident report on him, and he was locked away in segregation. Some inmates attending the service later said they had no clue what he was doing or why I was throwing him out. But others got the word out that I wouldn't tolerate that kind of nonsense.

I wouldn't recommend my direct method to volunteers. Depending on the circumstances, I recommend a member of your group exit the study and get the chaplain or an officer. But in my role as chaplain, I needed to send a message. I liken it to the tactic of Jesus taking the whip and casting out the moneychangers from the temple. In my case, throwing him out in front of everyone was risky. Inmates have their own system of justice for perceived disrespect. Inmate justice could have very well been served up to him for disrespecting me as well as the inmates attending their religious services. But in the jail and prison environment, you can't allow the depravity of one to destroy what others are receiving through the chapel service or religious study.

I know some reading this are rolling their eyes regarding my puritanical perspective on touch in jail and prisons. Many of you come from denominations where the laying on of hands is engrained within your prayer for others and hugs, regardless of gender, is part of your fellowship. Listen. As a professional chaplain working with male inmates, even I had faithful male inmates on the ministry team receive other inmates who needed prayer when giving alter calls. Alter calls require the lingering hand grasp and leaning in to listen in confidence to a person's heart, making even that kind of touch same-sex mandatory and wise in that setting. Use touch intelligently when working with the incarcerated. Please don't ignore this warning. This advice will at least invoke some wise thought behind the physical touch rather than just acting on impulse. Yes, sometimes, these inmates need a hug or handshake of encouragement. But always work from the plumb line, not the exceptions.

CHAPTER 17

Be in Charge—Beware of Inmate Pastors

I remember the first day on the job at one of the prisons where I worked. The self-appointed inmate *pastor* of a certain group came and introduced himself. He proceeded to give me his *credentials* and all he was doing in the chapel endorsed in the past, he said, by other chaplains. I was encouraging, but I chose not to plug into his implied request for my endorsement of whatever role in leadership he wanted. While I engaged his faithfulness in various chapel programs, I did not abdicate my role as teacher/shepherd in the chapel. Because of that, during the course of my tenure at that prison, he went from totally supportive of chaplaincy programs to actively speaking against my ministry and trying to sow discord among the chaplains and other inmates. He went so far as to generate a campaign advocating for him and his followers to take over chapel services with me as just a monitor.

What caused the flip-flop? I believe he began to become a backbiter and lose his way because, while his identity was entrenched in his newly found faith, he was skipping vital stages of his growth. New believers, especially those coming out of egregious trauma in their lives, don't understand that part of their journey of sanctification is learning to be still and listen to the teachers God places in their lives. It is necessary for their faith walk to be framed on resting in the irrevocable relationship with God and not their ability to measure up by endless activity to prove their faithfulness to God and others.

You as volunteers help them in that journey. However, you'd be surprised how many volunteers play the part of faux senior pastor when they come in and let the inmates organize and run the whole service with the volunteer just doing the main sermon, and sometimes not even that. They allow an inmate, often seen as the jailhouse preacher, to set the tone and format and end up sitting in the audience, letting the inmate run the study. Not good.

You don't see what chaplains see on a daily basis. Far too many inmate jailhouse preachers have their epiphany in their relationship with God and interpret that as a calling to preach the gospel. They hungrily seek a formal platform to openly share the gospel in a public way. Inmates who have found a new faith or, at the other extreme, are good at playing church often integrate themselves into leadership positions with a volunteer service that all but makes a spectator of that volunteer. Religion is one of the few places in their incarceration that empowers them personally, and they often confuse that newfound feeling of self and belonging by interpreting it as a form of calling. They seek a platform to express it. While the motive is most often compelled by their desire to be vocal for the Lord, their application is faulty.

Volunteers, when you are approved to come into the prison or jail, there is a reason. The chaplain or administration has certain expectations of you. You aren't being approved to come in just to keep the inmates company. You are to come in and fill a void where inmates are self-teaching. It's okay to have a teaching or worship format that may include inmates who regularly attend your program, but there's one thing you should never do. You should never just come in to be a figurehead. Let me make it perfectly clear. Do not let the inmates run the services or the bible studies when you are in attendance. Why are you even coming into the prison if all you are going to do is sit and listen to an inmate teach or preach? If you do not have something to teach the inmates you are serving, then do not come in.

Why would inmate leadership in religious areas be a problem? Isn't it always good when God's people who are incarcerated bloom where they are planted and minister within their bondage? Of course, and that's even wholesome. But remember: jails and prisons are a cloistered situation with numerous other dynamics at play. And while many inmates who are people of faith want to practice their religion peacefully while incarcerated, others get twisted in their application and mix personal ego or political grievances using their religious platform to push at the system. Most facilities do not even allow inmate run group activities unless closely supervised especially in teaching situations. It's a fundamental security issue. Giving an inmate that power allows a type of organization and the ability to coordinate on command the behavior of that group. That's dangerous to the security of the jail or prison. The search for free world volunteers to assist in programming efforts for every religious practice is not just for political show. It serves as a balance in the institution.

Still not convinced? More examples. One religious group has basic military roles in the free world that include ranks and authority. If allowed in prison, they would do drills and salute each other in a pseudo paramilitary practice. I've known individuals from this group to challenge staff and the system by calling for help from members of their group to resist staff when they have breached a rule and are being taken to segregation. They also incorporate various intimidation methods to block entry of nonmembers and even staff during programming. Do I really need to explain why allowing an organized military-type religious practice inside a prison is asking for trouble? Having a volunteer from their community most often rids the group of power struggles and misapplications of their religious practices.

While non-Christian groups have the reputation of the more aggressive behavior, individual Christian inmates gain followings and compete for authority with volunteers and chaplains, even so far as to bad-mouth those volunteer or chaplain lead services they see as competition to their ability to lead a program. I've had those misguided people actually stand outside volunteer or chaplain programs trying to dissuade their peers from attending. Remember: everyone tries to find that group to identify with when incarcerated, from street gang to religious group. This is not so hard to understand when you remember the human dynamic of people needing family and a place of acceptance while doing their time. Inmates who reject gang affiliation for safety and support will often turn to their religious group and form clichés for safety and emotional support. There's always an inmate religious leader, but that shouldn't translate to you transferring unassigned organization to them when you come in to offer your time.

To clarify, it doesn't mean you can't facilitate inmates participating and having roles in your worship service or study. Regular prison teams with enough volunteers usually have things planned out from music to sermon. However, sometimes, a solo minister will come in to do the service or study and appreciate inmate participation in the music leadership and format of the service. There's nothing wrong with assigning inmates who are regulars to your program to a segment of the service, but it should always be at your direction. And you should do the preaching or teaching. Period.

Let me flush another rabbit. If you are inclined to pick inmates to organize your services, just be careful. You are in danger of unknowingly perpetuating some pretty petty jealousy issues if you set up one inmate over another to organize and dole out worship program responsibilities to other inmates. To be frank, many inmates complain to chaplains when they come to hear a volunteer and an inmate does the teaching or is in charge. They want that outside free world influence and teaching and resent it when an inmate takes that role. They want *you* to teach, not another inmate. There are all kinds of tentacles that can ignite tension in these situations.

Every service should begin and end with you in the leadership role. That spiritual zeal coming from a changed man or woman is wonderful. But the *process* of sanctification is something you will need to call to their attention through your teaching. That means inmates should take full advantage of the teaching of a volunteer or chaplain when they are available and not seek to take over that role. There are no quick fixes in their pilgrimage. An inmate may be versed in scripture but not have the wisdom of application under his belt. God uses *your* ministry to disciple them. They must get knowledge of scripture, then understanding of the meaning of the scripture, and God then puts it all together by giving them wisdom for how to apply such in all circumstances under His umbrella of grace. Volunteers need to be in the driver's seat with their program format. You have to take on the role for which you are coming into the prison or jail in the first place. You can't acquiesce to an inmate who sees himself as the next Billy Graham or is trying to make up for lost time. That's your purpose as a minister in prisons and jails. Be in charge.

SECTION TWO

Spiritual Traps in Jail and Prison Ministry

CHAPTER 18

Be Aware of Jailhouse Religion

Jailhouse religion. It's commonly associated with an inmate who is using religion maliciously to play the system. But not all jailhouse religion is bad. Some is just part of their journey to faith. A lifetime of experience working with the incarcerated has helped me break down several kinds of missteps incarcerated people have in trying to find peace through their faith while locked up. I'll attempt to address it, but, to be real, this subject would fill a whole book.

I had a rude awakening early on with jailhouse religion while working in a large county jail. This young woman had hooked up with a man who had committed a horrific murder. He was looking at the death penalty. She was looking at her own death sentence as a coconspirator. She was housed in a segregation unit because of the high-profile nature of the crime. She had no bond. I made a point of visiting with her over the months of her pretrial. She often voiced her regret and repentance for her actions. She studied the lessons I gave her, and we had some very in-depth counseling sessions on what brought her to this moment in her life.

I was driving in to work one day and heard on the local news she'd made a plea deal, probably turning state's evidence against her codefendant. She had received only five years, a far cry from the death penalty. Ultimately, she had only a couple of more years left to her sentence because of time served. I made my regular visit to her that day, expecting her to be thanking God for that miracle. I barely got my initial greeting out of my mouth when she literally proclaimed, "Oh, hi, Chaplain. Thanks, but I don't need you anymore." Seriously, those were her actual words, and they are seared in my brain.

I said okay and wished her well, turned around, walked down the range, and was buzzed out of segregation. I stood on the other side of that door stunned and, frankly, very angry. I had spent a lot of time with this woman and was being discarded like a gum wrapper. I commiserated to God silently, telling him how ill-used I'd been and all the time I had wasted. Then God whispered, "Why are you so angry? She did this to me, not you." It was a bucket of water in the face. That wake-up call was one of the moments in my ministry that again reminded me I'm not in control of a person's choices or their relationship with God. All I can do is bring the message.

It was a hard lesson in one form of jailhouse religion. I had merely been her emotional crutch. The person pulls you in by seeming to pay attention to everything you are saying. Do you ever know if someone is playing you? No, you don't. We are called to go and share the gospel. What they do with the message is between them and God. If you remember that, you won't get cynical. God taught me through that experience, reminding me again about human behavior and myself. I reset. I learned to weigh time and investment with any one inmate based on their willingness to work on their own lives. I learned to give homework, initially with those who wanted long-term counseling to see how invested they were in their own relationship. In other words, I learned not to invest time into someone if they showed less desire than me to work on their lives. I was reminded not to allow people to recycle their stories of pain and use me as just another place to vent in a practiced cycle of dumping their emotional garbage, using people up, and moving on vent to someone else.

When do you know if an inmate has had a real "conversion"? Let me make this clear right off the bat, you never do. Assessing a person's sincere conversion is not in your power, nor is it your job. Your goal is spreading the gospel, not keeping tabs on numbers of conversions. Don't fall into the numbers trap, and you'll be more apt to discern when a person is on an emotional conversion trip, a calculated play for some other kid of support from you or an actual conversion.

I get the need to find gauges to determine whether an inmate is just using you as an emotional crutch. We like to see some results, don't we? But remember, you are essentially missionaries, and years are spent planting seeds, and, sometimes, others see the harvest. You may never see the endgame.

But there are a few things that can measure a person's sincerity in their commitment to their faith and change. Publically professing their faith and willingness to be baptized, consistent changes in attitude and behavior, a measure of discipline in personal religious studies, taking responsibility for their previous actions and present shortcomings, and not blaming others are some evidences. It's what we all want to see as a measure in our relationship with God. But please get educated and understand the forms of jailhouse religion. It will keep you from putting people into timelines for evidence of overcoming habits or thought processes. Yes, James says faith without works is dead being alone. But, ultimately, that's between the person and God. It's his role to build holiness in a person through a lifelong relationship with them.

CHAPTER 19

The Spiritual Psychology of Jailhouse Religion

I once walked into the phone monitoring area in a county jail I worked at. The correctional officer called me over and had me listen. The phone conversation was vile. The CO turned to me with a snide grin and said, "Know who that is?" I shook my head no. He then named an inmate known for his religious zeal on the compound. I suppose he thought I'd be surprised. But I wasn't. I said, "Well, I suppose he has some more growing to do, huh?" But that encounter enforced why there's such cynicism regarding conversions in jails or prisons. While you may see them with their bibles every time you come in to do a study with them, back in their lockers, they may have sexual literature, are adept at gambling, or speaking foul language, and the officers and the other inmates see that disparity.

Jailhouse conversion skepticism is foundationally based on the false premise that a person who has that encounter with Christ will never make a mistake again. Wrong. Just because an inmate may revert to some long-held behavior does not mean they didn't have a sincere profession of faith. Sanctification is a process. But how do you combat the skepticism that comes from staff and inmates and sometimes even yourself regarding jailhouse religion? I'd say just beware of the dynamics and be ready if necessary to explain the nuances of conversions in a prison setting if the subject comes up with staff or even free world friends skeptical of your ministry.

Compare it to the birth of a child. The baby never gets unborn but has a lot of growing to do. It's a journey of relationship. Control over go-to habits is part of the sanctification work in progress. An inmate who banks on the instant fix isn't in relationship with God. They are in want of some mindless miracle pill that doesn't require the relationship or the process of healing. They have to stop holding on to a perception of a Jesus whose love depends on their efforts. Instead, they need to let Jesus hold on to them. It's much like the difference in a child taking the hand of a parent rather than the parent taking hold of the hand of the child. If the child holding the hand of the parent stumbles, he will let go to catch himself and might fall headlong. However, when a parent takes hold of the child and the child stumbles, he may skin his knee, but the strength of the parent keeps him from doing a face-plant. The parent may chide the child to watch where they are going, which is a call for personal responsibility, but it doesn't negate parent and child bloodlines.

There are basically three types of *jailhouse religion* I've encountered: the Intentional Manipulator, the Sincere Seeker, and the True Follower. Ask the Lord for discernment in these matters.

The Intentional Manipulator is the one whose tactics result in most of the skepticism regarding religious converts in prison.

This person uses religion as a means to gain deliverance, but not the deliverance found in relationship with God. They seek to manipulate you to try to get them to do something for them, such as deliver a letter, make a call to family or an attorney, or pass along some information outside the regulations set up in the jail or prison. Some just use you to fill their time and maybe get a boost to their emotions. They come to as many religious programs as possible and become a familiar face. They intently listen and participate in worship services and bible studies. They join in very emotional displays of worship in response to your services. They are really good at playing church. They compliment your teaching and stroke your ego by telling you how much it means to them that you are volunteering your time in the jail or prison. They intently absorb your counsel. They share their tragic story that got them where they are and thank you for bringing them to hope in Christ. Then, having sucked you in with compliments, they hit you up for that favor. They do that sometimes in such a way you think it was your idea. They are using religious participation to further their agenda. Involvement in religious programs is their ticket to a character reference in their file or a good word to the judge or the parole board or even to being left alone by a gang from which they are trying to disassociate. Religious programs are seen as a tool of survival. Volunteers are just another medium to use and bait for their own use. Once you turn them down, they stop coming to your meetings.

Those practicing this type of jailhouse religion are essentially the scammers of the street bringing their scams into the prison chapel setting. They have no problem in trying to con a religious volunteer or a staff member. They have not changed the behavior that brought them to prison because that's not their goal. Their free world behavior just continues when they come to prison. It's the life they've chosen, and they intend to stay at the top of the food chain in prison. It's all about survival and power. It's survival, in that they have found a vent for their emotional system with volunteers and emotional religious services; and power, in that they have found a forum to stage their personal agenda using religious liberties already in place. They simply merge.

The second kind of jailhouse religion is the Sincere Seeker using formula-based measurements. Most of the people that are in our prisons, while having some experience with religion on the outside, never really understood what *relationship* with God was about. They embrace their newfound or rededicated faith. They are trying to find some relief from all their mistakes and associated guilt for failures and have an earnest desire to get their life turned around. The causational emotional dynamics are the same with these types of inmates: separation from family, off the drugs, titles and power taken away. These people really do want to change, but being ignorant of the principles of the gospel, they replace the empty holes in their lives with religious formulas. God becomes their painkiller. Religious practice fills a void and gives them something to hold on to while incarcerated. I don't think this kind of jailhouse religion is intentional, just uneducated. They don't seem to keep from trying to help God clean up their lives. For them, that translates to never measuring up to perceived expectations they think God has of their progress. Grace is secondary to works. This type of jailhouse religion plays out with the inmate getting into God, not God getting into them.

When a person practices a religion based on formulas, it ultimately becomes disappointing to the point of disenchantment. Religious practice takes on a type of magical evoking of God. "See, God, I'm doing all You say. Now help me get out of this mess." It relies on the power of the inmate's ability to interpret and even redefine faith as a *guess at what God wants.* It places them right back into the mold of trying to measure up that they may have been following all their life. They feel that if they follow God completely, then God must do what they ask of Him. When one religious practice doesn't work, and they don't see immediate tangible results or a reduction of their pain, they try another. "Maybe I'm not praying enough," they say, or "Maybe if I follow all the traditions of the Old Testament to the letter, or "If I just wear this religious necklace or this religious hat and looked religious, if I stand firm in my beliefs even against the system, maybe God will see I'm trying hard and help me out of prison or at the least help me to survive my time."

The Sincere Seeker engages in no more than a disciplined legalistic regimen and a stiff relationship with a distant god who has to be appeased by right actions. This is the "form of godliness" the New Testament talks about, with no power to help them lastingly change. They don't get the idea that it's relationship, not religion, they are looking for. It's a legalistic formula approach to conversion in prison relying heavily on how good they are at measuring up to what they perceive as God's expectations. The problem is the inmate can never quite get the formula right. And for many, great disillusionment sets in when their gauge of spiritual accomplishment fails them. They do not always see their case overturned. Their spouse goes ahead and leaves them. Their appeal for shorter sentencing doesn't work. This gets them deeper and deeper into self-condemnation and despair.

The struggle is real for the Sincere Seeker of relationship with God. If the foundations aren't laid correctly, such as teaching the reality that their walk is a learning experience throughout their life, which includes getting on God's timing, they ultimately have many setbacks, toss their Bibles, and go back to what was working before to get some emotional relief. Back come the drugs, the gangs, whatever their dependency of choice. Now, they have an additional failure to add to their repertoire. They feel they are just not what God is looking for and can't seem to connect with God. They leave religion behind with the feeling that there is no hope for them. They conclude that not even God can help them.

Finally, we come to the True Conversions. When people have that encounter with Christ, we rejoice in their breakthrough birth. Don't confuse leading them in the sinner's prayer as evidence of an actual conversion. Yes, those words of commitment start their open commitment. But those words of their need for God and repentance of their sin are also only a formula if not followed by the understanding that it is God who transforms and they begin their journey of relationship. Be aware: there's really no explaining someone else's experience of birth. We recognize what is happening, but it is for them that moment they enter into that light of relationship and start their walk with Him. We only have their profession of faith to go on and can measure attitude and behavior changes to a degree. It's their fruit that will tell the story over time.

But not many volunteers will maintain a lifetime of involvement with people they encounter in prison ministry. If we have more dealings with them before they are released, we begin to disciple them with grounding scripture and models of support. We can be available for questions and help them to discern personal discipline, which are action choices that stem from learning to love God back, away from legalism that is measured by rules and regulations.

These inmates approach their conversions much like Martin Luther when beginning his search for truth. While studying the book of Romans, Martin Luther finally had that light bulb experience that faith alone saves us apart from our own good or bad works. Salvation is completed by Christ on the cross apart from our help. But faith alone does not mean the absence of works. It simply means the finished work of Christ on the cross alone is foundational to any reason to even do good works or choice to turn away from temptation. We love God because He first loved us. Our relationship with Him is simply learning to love God back. Help them know that.

If we don't have the opportunity to follow up with a recent convert, it's hard. We commit to prayer those true converts and leave them to God. We pray that God will bring others in their lives along their life's journey to mentor them. The important thing with those temporary encounters is to make sure they know to read their Bible, pray, and stay around others who are on the same journey. Basic literature helps a lot, but the best thing to recommend to them is to read the gospels. Learning who Jesus is from four angles is grounding for them. Then you have to leave them to God.

Some larger prison ministries have new believer's courses and studies and even spiritual academy classes weekly in prisons. But when that's not possible, besides the "manual" itself, God's Word, I recommend Francis Schaeffer's unique book, *25 Basic Bible Studies.* There are also Prison Fellowship programs and studies; Campus Crusade for Christ studies; books like *It's Not About You* by Max Lucado, which centers them on relationship and the big picture; and *A Tale of Three Kings* by Gene Edwards, which is an allegorical study in brokenness. You probably have study tools that have helped you and can recommend. But the bottom line is that a true conversion sets in motion a lifelong journey of study and relationship.

I'm not advocating you check off the boxes to determine the sincerity of a person's conversion. Just beware that the only one to really determine a person's motives and conversion is God. Just keep these types of jailhouse religion in mind as you minister. Your role is to present the gospel and disciple, encourage, and correct as you have opportunity to impact individual lives.

CHAPTER 20

Stay Principle Based when Teaching in Jails and Prisons

No amount of time spent in prison or jail ministry is wasted. However, listen closely to what I am about to say. There is an art to sharing the gospel in jails and prisons. You are spinning your wheels if you primarily lay foundations of *victory* rather than the *principles* of the scripture.

According to *Webster, a principle* is "a fundamental, primary or general law or truth from which others are derived." Contrast that definition with *victory,* which is defined as "a success or superior position achieved against any opponent, opposition, or difficulty."

Don't get me wrong. I'm not saying it's wrong to share personal victories with the inmate. Everyone is encouraged and inspired by victory stories. But be careful, don't get top heavy on those stories. If you try laying lasting spiritual foundations based on your victories, it's only a glorified pep talk. Pep talks can rally a person's emotions momentarily but have no ability to fuel any lasting cure for what troubles them. Their present struggle should ultimately always lead them back to their own personal relationship with Holy God, not some comparison with your story.

Victory-oriented application of the gospel is the chief reason for shallow jailhouse religion. Many inmates are sponges for the victorious stories volunteers share at bible studies and worship services. Some inmates come for the feel-good emotions they get when volunteer groups come in. Inmates leave these services very encouraged, emotionally charged, and within a day of some great revival service, the high leaves, and they are left with nothing but their old problems and a sense of personal failure once again.

Dealing with the incarcerated is a ministry to those who are living 24-7 in crisis. There is a huge temptation to want to relieve that pain. Yes, we are to encourage and edify. These people have been ridden hard and put up wet. They are emotionally exhausted by anger, despair, betrayal, repeated failures, and traps of their own making. Who wouldn't want to share that there is a light at the end of the tunnel and at least help them come up for air in their struggles by sharing personal victories with those still in the mire? We got to the other side of the river, and we want to tell them how we did it. But it's not *your* victories that will enable them to have a relationship with Christ. It's the principles of faith you followed and the relationship you developed. When sharing, don't leave that fact hanging. Many are the product of our quick-fix society. Don't play into that in how you present the gospel.

As you consider your bible studies and worship services, take a moment somewhere to convey the spirit of the old adage, "It's not how high you fly but how straight you walk when you hit the ground." And, sometimes, that straight walk is long, boring, and full of wolf traps. A person doesn't hop from one mountaintop to another. There are valleys of learning between those mountaintops. There are things about relationship with the Almighty that can only be learned in the valley. A valley has its own beauty even when it's dark. Prepare them for that.

The encounter with God that is life-changing is a process led by the Holy Spirit. You can't put the real thing on a fast track. You may be further along in the sanctification process, but they are yet on their journey through areas you've already crossed. Don't take away the ability for them to take their own journey by running past them in your haste to share your personal victory with the purpose of making them feel better. The "I did it, and you can too" message may cause them to measure their own victories by yours. That can handicap them right at the start of their walk. Yes, share a relevant victory, but meet them where they are. Point them to everyone's standard of measure, Christ.

Trust me, if they spend time in the Word and in relationship with God, that peace in their storm will come. It's in that familiarity with the personal God that fear gives way to peace when all around them is chaos. The greater joy for you is in knowing the Lord is using you *in that process*. You are one step in that person's encounter with God and perhaps ultimate decision for salvation and His continuous sanctification process in their life. The process of God making us holy is not just knowing God but having relationship with Him. It probably won't model yours. It's not supposed to. Principle-based ministry feeds the victories. It's important to lay foundations of principle and hold tight to that, for it is in those grounded foundations that spiritual victories are won.

CHAPTER 21

Don't Teach Cheap Grace

This may appear to be similar to that last chapter, but it goes down its own path. Over the years, I've known inmates who mistakenly conclude that once they repent and follow Christ, it's only a matter of time where their sentence will be shortened or commuted. When this doesn't happen, their faith takes a hit. It causes them to revert to judging themselves by a failure to measure up and being good enough for anyone to love, much less God.

Unfortunately, many volunteers either purposefully or unwittingly teach this falsity that once a person has accepted Christ as their Savior, the fix is in for the quick fix from their sentence and addictions. This false belief sets them up for their faith to crash and burn when the doors fail to open or their addiction overwhelms them again. God, of course, can do what He wants and instantly deliver a person from addictions. But even then, He works from there establishing a personal relationship with the individual and building foundations of spiritual stability that create in that person the desire and ability to *continue* to overcome through the power of God. But, please, one size doesn't fit all. What God has planned for one pilgrimage may not be another's. Do not promise or infer that once they repent and have a relationship begin, God will knock those prison doors down. Remember, most all of the disciples were martyred.

Let me double down here. Prison ministry doesn't need people who have a soothsayer mentality in the delivery of the image of God that waves His magic wand and everything is fixed and the consequences of past actions will just go away. People need to take responsibility for their own actions. Repentance is not just saying you're sorry. Sorry doesn't fix anything. It just makes you feel better for a while. And sorry isn't a magic word that delivers from consequences. That person they may have murdered on a spree is still just as dead and their families devastated, those millions they embezzled from seniors still destroyed people's hopes for a secure old age, or those drugs they smuggled and sold down the pipeline still helped to create addictions in thousands.

It's important to teach the inmates the bigger picture. While God may, perhaps, swing those doors open sooner than later, it may also be in His will that they serve out their full term. Their mission field may be the prison, and the greatest faith is learning to rest in the Lord and be on mission whether they are in prison or in the free world. God first delivers the eternal spiritual man. While we long for a physical deliverance in our earthly situations, God is more interested in the process and the journey with Him as He continues to make us holy in that journey.

The old cheap grace game of you-scratch-my-back-I'll-scratch-yours is just another way of making "rice Christians." That's a phrase coming from the use of free rice by missionaries to gain converts in China. Isn't implying or even teaching that once they repent, all the consequences of their actions will magically go away just another version of the rice Christian tradeoff? As a volunteer, don't teach cheap grace. Otherwise, you're engaging in teaching them to barter with God. And when things they want don't happen, they crash and burn spiritually and emotionally.

Grace is favor not earned, and repentance is a godly sorrow perpetuated by the Holy Spirit, who then regenerates that person in union with God. This leads to power to want to turn away from sin in everyday life as God makes us holy. It is a love relationship that will enable them to succeed in spite of the storms of life and even fulfilling their entire sentence. We learn the nature of God. And getting to know Him, we learn to listen and rest in Him. That causes us to move forward in life in spite of past failures. That's what we pass on in sharing the gospel with inmates.

CHAPTER 22

The Trap of Epiphanies

Kin to cheap grace conversions and a victory-based gospel are nuances of epiphanies. An epiphany is the moment all the dots connect. For the incarcerated, it's that moment it dawns on them *why* they are making the bad choices that landed them in jail or prison. They let go of the blame game and take responsibility for their life. It's also often followed up with a deep resolve to make a change. That's a good thing, but beware of epiphanies. Though an epiphany can cause a person to change course for the better, they can fool a person into a proud religious place, and that often feeds on a temporary emotional religious experience. That produces nothing more than jailhouse religion.

If you've done prison ministry for any length of time, you can name people who were enthusiastic about their new faith. They came to every service and bible study. They were a key spiritual leader with their prison buddies, often holding prayer groups in the units. Most of the time, they were helpful to the chaplain or volunteer in dealing with chapel politics and really tried to seek the Lord in all their ways. You saw positive change and growth in them. Then they were gone. Sometimes, it was just a change in a prison job assignment that was used as the excuse. Other times, it was a small offense from another Christian that put them off, or the new just wore off, and when the walk and talk was challenged by tribulation, their expectations were shattered by false expectations of just how the Lord delivers a person.

Volunteers need to help inmates build their spiritual walk based on foundational teachings, not on some psychological epiphany that may result only in a course change in their lives, not a spiritual regeneration. It's like relying on the plug for power rather than the light socket. Don't be afraid to ask probing questions of a person professing faith.

When Jesus called the Pharisees *whitewashed tombs,* I think he was addressing those who had mistaken *religion* for relationship. Being aware of what contributed to taking the road that led them to prison is a starting point but doesn't fix the problem. Admission of guilt is not repentance. A dawning of how they got to this place in their life may give them a starting point, but it produces no power. Repentance comes from a sorrow when a person realizes they have violated relationship with God who loves them. True repentance leads to a hunger for fellowship with God and produces relationship that holds you up when you face life.

Beware of those living a jailhouse religion that just causes them to bleed out emotionally. Help them depart from just getting into God and being religious, and teach them about relationship and a lifetime of the process of sanctification. Teach them to let God get into them by developing that intimate relationship. Help them understand what relationship means. If they do that, then their walk becomes something personal, not just an epiphany bunch of dos and don'ts. Then it's a permanent fix. That scalpel of God will produce love, peace, patience, faith, and the ability to stay the course in their relationship with Christ throughout their lives. That and that alone will end the rotating doors that cycle them in and out of prison. You have to help them not stall out at the epiphany and move on to grace and start building their lives on the rock, not the shifting sand that life will throw at them.

Salvation by grace through faith is what our relationship with God is all about, and sometimes we need to be reminded of the simplicity of faith in Christ. But for these men and women to have some foundations that produce that steadfastness, it's up to us to help them understand sanctification, which produces order, discipline, and sound teaching for our steadfast walk throughout our lives. Otherwise, we contribute to their spiritual failure by omission.

We must lay the foundations well in these men and women or hear more sadness from family members regarding the failure of even one of the most faithful inmates in Christ when they get out. Here's a letter sent to a chaplain regarding such a failure. This inmate performed as a steadfast Christian leader in many chapel services and in the units. But his time would have been better served dealing with his own growth. Here's a wake-up call from a heartbroken mother who wrote a fellow chaplain about her son who had been released but was now on his way to being rearrested.

> Dear Chaplain,
>
> You were so helpful to my son when he was incarcerated there that I felt compelled to write to you. I hope you do not mind. My son resumed

> his old habit of crack cocaine after only 10 days of freedom. He had everyone fooled and we believed him when he said he was done with drugs. He went back on his promise to God, to his family, and also to himself. It is as if the old son never changed at all. It seems as if he is trying to make up for all the months that he could not do drugs. He has two years of supervised release, better known as probation, so do not be surprised if you look up one day and see his face. He has to undergo random drug testing. I appreciate all that you did for him when he was there. Please say a prayer on his behalf.

Without the growth a person needs, a mere life-changing epiphany is like an oak with shallow roots. The first big storm that comes along it topples over. It is like learning to saddle a horse without all the other nuances of knowing about the horse's personality or the techniques of riding. It's akin to owning a gun without having the bullets. It's like a ship altering its course to keep from going on the reef only to hand over the ship to a civilian who has no knowledge of how to steer in currents or changing waters. Ground them. Take them beyond epiphanies.

CHAPTER 23

Spiritual Vocabulary

Don't presume people understand even the most common spiritual words, doctrines, or even definitions of words and concepts. Help them to reframe their thinking so they can build on your topic. It's generally a good idea in any teaching moment to know your audience, but especially when dealing with inmates. Inmates come from all walks of life and religions or no religion at all. They also have different levels of education. Build on the elementary without being condescending.

There are basic definitions of everyday words that should be considered as well—for instance, the teaching of God as their Father. Many have fathers who are absent or who have failed in their role as a father. You may be thinking you are getting your point across with all the rapt faces staring at you, but their mind may have stopped at the word *father* and are entertaining some bad memories and never connect with the fatherhood of God you are trying to convey. The perfect attributes and concept of *father* should be defined if you are trying to help them understand the *fatherhood of God*. Maybe list attributes of a father so they build on the plumb line of what you are trying to teach them about God. A father is an integral part of a family, a role model, a gift giver, one who shows unconditional love, a disciplinarian, provider, a protector—all of which can be lessons in themselves. This approach peaks their attention to discovering for themselves what the fatherhood of God is like in their own studies. It diverts them to the true nature of a father rather than perhaps a bad image of a father they may have formed in childhood. It's not always a huge theology lesson, just a simple diversion to define and clarify so you can move on in your topic.

You should even go more elementary. What about just the basic word *God*? Explore that. When I teach, I explain that God is about revealing Himself to us as much as we humans can grasp. I may explain, without getting too deep, that the English language is not as descriptive as the Greek or Hebrew. The English just says God. In the Hebrew, God's actions are defined by names that describe His characteristics.

For instance, there are fourteen descriptive names of God in Hebrew. A study of where these words are used in the scripture is an awesome study on the personality of God allowing him to describe Himself. I may pick one like *El Roi,* to illustrate. It's used in Genesis 16:13 and is a proclamation of gratitude for protection. Nahum 1:7 reads, "You are God who *sees* me! The Lord is good, a stronghold in the day of trouble and *He knows those who take refuge in him.*" He sees you. Many inmates don't feel seen or heard by God. This personalizes Him by description. So, if you are teaching about God, it's prudent to discuss what description or action of God is being used *in the particular* verse being used. That will stick to their brain and start them thinking in detail about God.

The point is you aren't just scattering chicken feed when you teach in jails and prisons. Pay attention, and take some care every time you go in to do a study. Who is your audience? What is it that group needs? Yes, you have a topic, but take care you remember that what is common terminology to you may not be heard with the same ears you have.

CHAPTER 24

Preparing Inmates for Release

Inmates are scared to death of getting out, though they paradoxically chomp at the bits the closer that out date nears. High hopes flourish in their hearts for success. There's no way they want to make the same mistakes again. But the deck is stacked against them from the start. They are going from the condensed society of not being able to even decide what clothes they wear, who their cellmate is; never being able to deeply sleep for fear of their life; being told when to get up, what to eat, when to recreate, when to work, what property they can keep in their lockers, having limited access to commissary, to having to fend for themselves in all things upon release. They have to find jobs in a society that is skeptical of hiring ex-offenders. They have to find a place to live, transportation, and learn how they fit back into society. They have to restore or fit back into relationships with family, if any are left, who have passed them by in life experience and find their place in that family once again. Released inmates have even shared one of the most overwhelming events is just the simple act of going into a supermarket and being presented with the hundreds of choices of food. One former inmate said he had to leave the market, it was so overwhelming. Tremendous stress hits them in every direction right upon their release.

When all is said and done, all your efforts inside bringing the gospel to the inmates are hopefully to give them a head start on the outside. Prepare inmates for the free world not only with optimism but also with reality. While their newfound or refreshed relationship with God is their foundation, it should not be divorced from the everyday reality of the obstacles that will meet them as they exit incarceration. But the Lord will be with them every step of the way.

- Teach them they will be met with skepticism. Teach them to validate themselves by God's standard, not by seeking approval of others. They've probably already heard the sarcastic remark that all inmates get religion when they are locked up. That skepticism will follow them out the door and take many forms. They will carry labels all their life. But that is what they have done, not who they are. That's why they should not gauge themselves by what people say or how society categorizes them. They have to counter labels and a feeling of hopelessness with what God thinks of them. Not to say they shouldn't do proper restitution, if possible, as God leads them, but they cannot go back and undo or fix things. That's not where they should put their energy. They must accept what is, take responsibility, and set a path to make sure they don't go down that same trail. Setting that path in its simplest form is personal bible study and prayer, a person to be accountable to who is not from their family, finding a church, getting a job, and finding things to do that lets them enjoy their life. And, yes, God does want them to enjoy their life and not constantly doing penance for things God already has forgiven them for. They should keep their eyes on the eternal goal, take each step of their journey one at a time, and not set timelines especially through the eyes of other's expectations.

- Teach them to guard their heart. What they read and watch affects their thinking. They should create a daily pattern of bible study that works for them. Good foundational verses to bring to their attention are Philippians 4:6–9 and Proverbs 4:23. These verses instruct them to pray about everything, letting God know what they need as well as thanking Him for what He has already done. God promises, if they do that, peace at the unknown will fill their hearts as they pursue the things of life. It also instructs them to trust God with their whole selves, not relying on their own human understanding, trusting God to bring what they need to pass, and peace will fill their hearts even when they see nothing on the horizon. God can, out of the blue, take care of us, and when God fulfills our request with that exhibition of God's immeasurable grace, it builds our faith and walk with Him.
- Getting a job won't be easy. Skepticism for the hiring of felons is the resistance they may experience when looking for a job. Some former inmates have skills that make the hunt a bit easier; others don't. There is an innate fear from employers of former inmates at any level. That can lead them to despondency and a chipping away of their resolve because they have to fight that labeling every time they apply for a job.

Teach them to be honest on their application. A simple "will explain" on the line where it asks if they've ever been incarcerated will allow them to explain their story face-to-face to an employer and add as much or as little of the circumstances of their history. Their honesty about their past may make points with their potential employer enough for them to take a chance on employing them. Many former felons have been willing to start at any job, been faithful, and climbed up the ladder of success.

- Teach releasing inmates not to make promises, not even to their families. Their actions are what have impacted their family in the first place, and it's their actions that will impact relationships when they release, not another promise they feel they have to live up to. They should seek to live up to their faith in God, not promises others have always heard. They should commit to the Lord and themselves. Any change to bad habits that have tripped them up should not be changed for another person, but because it honors God and their relationship with Him. That may sound selfish, and it is in a principled way. If they do what they need to do to get spiritually and physically healthy, that will produce behavior that will ultimately impact their relationships in a lasting way with their friends and family and society as a whole.
- Warn them that the walk of a Christian can get lonely and may tempt them to seek out old friends. They may have to endure a type of isolation because of their desire not to repeat their mistakes. They'll have to make new friends or decide to learn to be alone.

Many well-intentioned former inmates have a burden for their friends and go around them initially with a desire to share what changed their life. They shouldn't translate that burden into permission to take their eyes off their own spiritual growth in a manner that turns them into another's rescuer. Being around others who are not committed to change in their life will poison their progress. When encounters with old friends occur, they should share the gospel, but not hang out. Believe me, they will find old friends still caught up in their wolf traps who will be more apt to want to see them fail so as not to spot light their own failures.

When I teach classes to releasing inmates, I give this example. I have an inmate stand on a chair and another stand below him. I then ask the group what is easier: for this man to pull someone up on the chair with him or for the person standing below him to pull him down. Various answers are given. I then instruct the person standing on the chair to try to pull the man below up on the chair. As imagined, it's a futile struggle to pull him up on the chair even when the bottom inmate isn't resisting. Then I reverse it. I tell the man below to try to pull the man on the chair off. Without exception, he is easily pulled down. Why? The balance is off. And so it will be for them if they think they can associate in fellowship with old friends who are not on the same journey as they. The balance is off.

Being alone should be their friend, not their foe. Being comfortable with being alone is a good thing. It gives a person time to learn to hear God in the silence and get to know their self in a positive way. Learning to be alone is not the same as focusing on yourself and what you don't have in your life. Yes, that can be intense. Self-absorption can actually cause a deeper loneness because it has nowhere to go. Enduring the intensity of that kind of loneliness sometimes drives a person to seek any kind of company and lead to setbacks in their faith walk. Loneliness will exist, but they have to become totally dependent on God alone apart from any other relationship or lack of it in their lives. That's learning to be alone. It's in those alone times that the best reality of self is made. God speaks in the loneliness as they experience a relationship with the God of the universe that is all fulfilling. That's a principle that will work toward making them in charge of whom they allow in their life. They will learn the power of choice from a position of strength and contentment. Their selection of friends and lifestyle should be driven not by needing a space-filler person as a crutch. They must be as content being alone as being surrounded by people. They don't have to settle by keeping old friends that are still not decided on living a commitment to the Lord. It's a new freedom they will enjoy.

- Teach them that conflict in their life can be a positive thing and not necessarily a gauge that they are doing something wrong. Satan will produce conflict right out of the blue they had nothing to do with and try to alter their walk. It's about how they respond. Point them to the book of Timothy and the verses on suffering.
- Teach them to listen to counsel but to validate the counsel by the principle of the Word. The Holy Spirit will let them know if something is wrong with the advice. Not everyone offering advice is sent by God. But remember, advice is like a red flag. A red flag stops you to access the situation. Sometimes, a red flag is simply there to

slow you down for a treacherous curve that you are supposed to take more slowly. Sometimes, it's to warn you the bridge is out and you need to take a different way to your destination. Sometimes, it's a warning to a strategic retreat. And, sometimes, it's just a stopping point so you will be still and know He is God.

- Teach them the difference between joy and happiness. Happiness has to do with mood and can change with the weather. Joy is peace in the storm. It is a confidence of His love and presence.
- Teach them to default to remembering who they are in the Lord. They should not judge themselves by their failures but by their position in the Lord. They are royalty, beloved of the Father, an heir of salvation. They are loved right now, all God is ever going to love them, which is completely. His love is not conditional.
- Teach them they are not obligated to be the poster child for any church wanting to make them a trophy for redemption just because they are coming out of a life that sent them to prison. Unfortunately, some churches unwittingly make it harder for released inmates to move on without the label. They are always identified as an ex-offender. They should not be expected to constantly wear that label no more than an adulterer, former drunkard, thief, liar, embezzler, etc. should. They need to move beyond the label and live their life, for all have sinned and fall short of the glory of the Lord. Whether they use their past as an example to help others not go down that road is totally up to them.

- Finally, teach them it's okay to enjoy their life. While discipline in studying God's Word and praying and church attendance is foundational, God expects us to enjoy His creation. There is nothing in scripture that says we have to walk around like we've been vaccinated with pickle juice. We were created for His pleasure, and He enjoys seeing us play. He created us with our own talents and interest, such as hobbies, fishing, old cars, horseback riding, training dogs, gardening, fixing cars, reading, woodworking, spending time with family, cooking and eating, whatever gives them joy that is from God. He loves to hear us laugh.

SECTION THREE

Essays That Teach: Real People Applied Principles

Though I won't name names, these essays are based on real encounters with inmates and the things God taught me through that encounter.

CHAPTER 25

Swinging from the Bars

"I found my thrill on Blueberry Hill!"

She sang it with gusto while swinging from the bars like a monkey. I was on my rounds in the segregation unit in a large county jail. She was the first cell on the left, so there was an immediate decision to be made: ignore her behavior or join in. I joined in. Well, why not? I liked the song. The steel walls were a natural sound reflector that acted like a sound system. Her rendition echoed down the range, sparking both laughter and backup singers among her peers. My joining in the song encouraged the ensemble, and for a short period, what is ordinarily a long row of separate cells housing disciplinary problems within the jail became a happy little songfest.

Blueberry Hill lady ended her take on the song in a particularly long note and a flourish, with her clinging to the topmost bars of her cell. The party came to an end. It quieted down pretty quick as reality zoomed back in on the women in the cages. She climbed nimbly down from the bars, a smile remaining on her face. This obviously was not her first rendition from her perch. There was a skepticism displayed in a smirk on her face as she landed in front of me. She was surprised her behavior had not put me off. It usually did and kept people from talking to her by design. Coo-coo had been working as her escape from pain for a long time. Not this time. We didn't get into anything particularly deep. We just chatted, and I prayed with her before I continued down range. I don't know about her, but I'd had a good time and left the range pretty upbeat.

Weeks later, I was at my church, the so-called seminary high church I was attending at the time. When the meet-and-greet time came in the service, we all proceeded to shake hands, greeting other members and visitors. A well-dressed attractive woman walked up to me and shook my hand.

"You don't remember me, do you?" she said, smiling, lingering in the handshake.

I had to admit I didn't as I looked intently at her, trying place her.

"I found my thrill on Blueberry Hill," she sang, conversationally leaning in. I was speechless. She thanked the astonished me for talking to her that day. The method had always put off people like me, and when I joined in her song, she felt like somebody just liked her for herself. She had done a lot of thinking after I left and found the strength to go back to her Christian roots and just turn things over to the Lord and quit the charades in her life. All that from me singing "Blueberry Hill" with her? Go figure.

Ministry to inmates is not always sharing the four spiritual laws or the Roman road, the faith talking points or three circles. It's often just meeting them where *they* are in their lives, not where *we* are, and letting the presence of God do His work in His own way. At times, we will have the opportunity to lead someone to Christ when it's time. But don't put God in a box.

Sometimes, God has "Blueberry Hill" and a segregation row concert in His repertoire.

Oh, and on another note, you never really know whom you are sitting next to in church. That well-dressed person sitting beside you just might have been swinging from the bars in a jail cell just a few days before. Even the disciples did time. But that's another subject, I suppose.

CHAPTER 26

Happy-Go-Lucky

He was a happy-go-lucky guy. He was trying to get a transfer closer to home, so he hadn't gotten any disciplinary write-ups in a while. A regular in the chapel, he knew all the answers. Literally, he thought he had it going on. He was a Christian, and his game was his religion. He participated in all the chapel services, dramas, bible studies, and regularly chatted with the chaplain. He had a funny sense of humor. He was entertaining to talk to. He could moralize with a sense of humor about his current situation, which, this time, had been going on for numerous years. He would come up with wonderful adages. I could use many as jumping-off illustrations in my sermons. One of my favorites was alluding to his attempts to clean up his life now that he was a Christian.

"Well, Chap," he said, grinning philosophically and leaning back in the chair across from me, "I may run upon the curb and lose a hubcap every now and then, but that wakes me up, and I get back on the road."

Great, huh? If only he didn't take so lightly his mistakes. He'd just laugh off his toe dipping into sin, not necessarily unrepentant, but not realizing that repentance means a godly sorrow at sin. People in pain sometimes soften it with humor, and that's not so bad if it doesn't turn into laughing off a lazy Christian's choice to give in to a sin.

A lot of these guys just substitute God as a painkiller for themselves. They are actually attempting a course change, but they use religion as a blueprint to attempt to steer the boat in another direction but with them still in control. Then they wonder why they keep getting sucker punched. It's because they never turn the steering over to God. Maybe it's because they get into God rather than God getting into them. And as long as they do that, they are just religious gaming. There's no power for change in that.

Funny guy got his transfer. About a year later, I heard he'd been found in a prison hallway half beaten to death. Guess someone didn't think he was so funny.

CHAPTER 27

Dreadlocks and Christ

He was a formidable black man with waist-length gray dreadlocks. It must've taken him years to grow them that long. I always wondered, cringing, how long it had been since they'd seen soap and water. He was an intelligent guy, and if you didn't believe it, hang around long enough and he'd tell you so. Though he was the strong leader in his religion, he had harnessed and blended several belief systems that allowed him to ensnare weak-minded inmates who followed their religion just enough to make them either miserable or troublemakers in the chapel. He taught a pluralistic faith mixed with strong measures of racial activism that made the practice of his Moorish Science Temple of America, an Islamic brand of religion, not entirely true to its roots. His take on it made it a mishmash of many religions with racism the primary focus, radicalism, and plain bad behavior as he applied it.

He was also pretty high up in his gang. Power and territory are major identity issues in prison, and because group activity is greatly curtailed, the only place these leaders can show personal influence in a group setting is as a religious leader among their own faith in the chapel. And he wore his power well, not afraid to come up against the chapel staff demanding rights and privileges far and beyond what could occur in a prison chapel setting. Standing against staff brought admiration from followers who were always looking for that person who would fall on their sword for the gang. He was comfortable with his role and wore it like a well-worn favorite pair of jeans.

I had numerous run-ins with this man. I always had to call on the Lord to give me wisdom and protect me physically. I engaged the system's disciplinary codes several times when he stepped over the line and watched as he was carted off by officers to the segregation unit for periods. You cannot back down from people who are commandeering the chapel for personal power issues. When he didn't cross the line verbally, I made many attempts to reason with him, even having religious discussions with him. I must have been able to keep up with him because he seemed to enjoy these dialogs on racism, politics, and faith. Honestly, I did too.

I always believe with my head that the Word of God will not be wasted on anyone. But, sometimes, I really wondered if anything ever got through to this guy at all because his habit was to keep the chapel in an uproar, inciting his religious group routinely over some perceived discrimination. He admired strength, which is a badge of courage to the inmates, and I could tell there was a grudging respect for me because I held his feet to the fire each time in a firm but fair manner. So even though I had to send him to the hole—the slang for disciplinary segregation—to his credit, he'd always come back and kept up the communication with me. But inmates like him always made my day tense, keeping me on alert.

Over time, I ended up working at the higher-level prison across the street. A year passed, and I had occasion to fill in for the chaplain that had taken my place at Dreadlock Man's location. I was standing in the office talking to an inmate chapel office worker when in walked Dreadlock Man. I acknowledged him with a nod and continued my conversation with the other inmate. I had a fleeting thought that I was sure glad I didn't have to wrestle issues with him anymore. He cordially listened to us and, when there was a break in the conversation, asked if I remembered him. I said of course with a smile and turned to face him. Before he could say anything else, the chapel inmate clerk happily spilled the beans.

"You know he's accepted Christ, don't you?"

On the outside, I didn't blink, smiled, and congratulated him, offering to hear his story. On the inside, I felt like the surprised Rhoda of the scripture, when she answered the door and found the answer to their prayers standing there, released from their prison by God. It was an ice-down-the-shirt moment. I felt the Lord chide me.

"Don't ever think even the most angry and confused man cannot come to know Me."

He reminded me when people fight so hard against God's people, chances are they are in the midst of a spiritual battle for their soul. No one can predict what a persons' final decision will be in relationship to God calling. We just have to be wise in our response, remember our mission, and hold the fort. We may or may not be treated to the joyful results on the other side of that person's encounter with Christ. But whether that's the case or not, just remember the old saying: God may be late, but He's always on time.

Dreadlock Man was a keen example of what God can do. Now, if He'd only help the guy deal with those dreadlocks. Sorry, not sorry. That hairdo just isn't a favorite of mine.

CHAPTER 28

The Sins of a Father

Thirty-eight years left to do in the joint. A lifetime. He will die in prison. This father speaks from the chaplain's office in prison to a son lying in a hospital bed somewhere in the free world, the results of being shot by in a drive-by. The son is feeling betrayed, sorry for himself, and angry, not understanding how close he came to dying. Interesting how people skip the obvious to lay blame elsewhere. The son's rage is apparent from the reaction of the face of the father talking to him. Lying in a hospital, snatched by the hair from death, and yet his son's only determination is to get well enough to return and wreak vengeance on the men that put him there. He's sold out, in a trap of his own making, a rationalization, an accepted lifestyle, a downhill spiral in sand too loose to get traction. It's a decision that will end in emotional, spiritual, and, eventually, physical death. It almost did this time. But he's not listening.

The father pleads with his son to straighten up, take responsibility for his actions, and let go of hate. The son continues to speak with this dad, but his physical pain merges with his bitter and vengeful heart. His father strains to hang on to any thread of influence he has left with his son. It is a long conversation of a father trying to pour into his son a warning and a lifetime of regrets. The plea of the father is intense, and I see him growing older and hunched as the son responds with accusations and determination to get even with the one who shot him. His anger is deeply rooted, and the pleas of his father bounce off him back into the broken heart of his dad. The years of living on the precipice, daring death, denying God flash in the dad's mind as the realization hits him that the sins of the father do impact the son. He tells his son he loves him and will pray for him. *Pray for him*—the phrase seems unfamiliar to him, the use of which is reaching into a place not visited much himself. He slowly hangs up the phone. The phone call has aged him visibly. He is silent, hunched, hands clasped, head down.

What do you say in a case like this? What words of comfort or encouragement will ease the pain of this father who has wasted his years pretending how he lived was his business and had no impact on his family, especially his sons? How does a man who will die in prison reach out to a son he has taught to hate and is following him down the same road to destruction? The man is imploding right in front of me. Seems futile.

That's when I realize once again no man comes to God unless it's God's idea. It is the Holy Spirit that can reach into the very pit of a man's hell and save his soul from death. It's that counsel I give this father, who says he has himself, in recent months, begun responding to the voice of God. I sense he is not far from the kingdom. But he does not accept Christ now. He is again teetering on a precipice, a position with which he is all too familiar. He can go either way. Perhaps God will use the love of this father for his son to cause him finally to say yes to Christ for himself. He is realizing that his son's only hope of being delivered from certain destruction is an intervention far beyond human counsel. He must first practice what he has just preached to his son. No longer can he hope his son will do as he says, not as he does. It's far too late for that.

He rises to go and leaves the office without making a decision. I pray silently on behalf of the father and son. The battle for the souls of these men is not over. It is in God's hands. It always is.

CHAPTER 29

Glorious Fear

Grandma's house always had that old musty smell even then. It was like stepping back in time every time we visited. The old house set upon stilts rested on top of a hill overlooking a busy country highway. The house always looked enormous to me and invited adventure. I was told Grandpa used to play the fiddle, and they'd have square dances in the parlor. Sometimes, I'd go into that room where the velvet brown carpet lay and twirl a dance or two myself.

At night, we'd vie for the intrigue of sleeping on the screened-in porch with Grandma in the feather bed. Most of the time, we'd all end up positioned somewhere on that bed, at the foot or sideways. It didn't matter. We might be uncomfortable, but we'd do anything to experience the glorious fear of the screened-in porch. I'd lie there oblivious to the others in the bed, snuggled. I'd be surrounded by mattress like a ball in a glove, too scared to move for fear some unknown creature would stick his hand through the screen and carry me off into the night.

The porch had it drawbacks, though. I really hated it when I woke up with nature calling. That meant a trek to the outhouse, a major pioneer journey, or a squat out the back porch, really exposed to the monsters. I always chose the quick dip into the night. At least I'd be close to the house when the monster killed me, and I'd be assured they'd find the body.

There were a lot of sounds I could identify while lying there in the darkness. But then there would be that one that would widen my eyes and make me stop breathing. I remember one particular night I woke up. Some night sound had startled me awake, I suppose. I moved my eyes slowly, trying not to move at all. That was not easy seeing as how I really had to go bad. There was something out there. It was big, and it just stood there looking at me. I knew if I didn't move, it wouldn't get me. So I lay there waiting, certain my time to be carried off was here.

I don't know how long I lay there having a stare out with the monster. Finally, light filtered out the night, and, gradually, the real world began to take shape. My monster materialized and turned out to be a clothesline pole. My body melted in relief. I jumped out of the comfy bed, dashed out the screen door, did my business, and scrambled back into the folds of the feather bed, thankful for all those chickens that had literally given the shirts off their backs. I snuggled deeper into the feather bed as the faint light of dawn gradually gave way to chirping birds and the smells of a new day. I drifted off into a very relieved sleep enveloped in Granny's feather bed.

Prison has its own nightmares and monsters. He hadn't always been a regular in the chapel. But, lately, he'd come to special events and was attending bible studies. Sometimes, he came to the regular worship services. He was a nice guy who was not particularly noticeable. But his peers seemed to like him and always included him in things. We had some interesting talks, all just conversations about new things he'd been learning about in the scripture. He started helping around the chapel doing odds and ends and just minding his own business doing his time., So when an opening came up for a worker in the chapel, we hired him. After one of the particularly well-attended worship services, he and another worker stayed after the inmate moved to finish cleaning. He and his friend were pretty happy, and I could hear them toss friendly banter at each other while they were cleaning. They finished, and I got them permission to cross the compound and head back to the unit.

The next day, I learned that this unpretentious inmate, upon entering breezeway to the unit, was assaulted and beaten up pretty badly. Seems earlier that day, he'd happened upon his cellmate's stash of home brew. His cellmate, a large intimidating man with an iconic teardrop tattooed under his eye, proof perhaps of a past kill, was afraid my chapel orderly was going to snitch and decided to do him in first.

The chapel inmate told me later he had never had a problem with the guy and had been his cellmate for a while. He'd probably never had trouble sleeping in the same cell. In this situation, he remembers walking in the cell earlier that day and noticed a smell but didn't think anything of it. He stated he had no clue the stuff was even there. The attacker had been provoked by his own fear of discovery and handled it the way he'd always handled it, by making the first strike. There was no way his victim could have predicted the attack.

That's the way it goes in prison. Everyone is living with his own monsters, fear being a big one. They can't even be sure when they lay their heads down to sleep that they will wake up in the morning. While we enjoy our glorious fears, which are often childish and benign, sleeping safely in our beds, inmates throughout our country are sleeping too, or trying to. It's amazing any of these guys get any sleep. The reality is, in prison, they have their dreams, and, at times, their nightmares become reality. When they are awakened, it's not some fantasy monster of a clothesline pole standing over them. It's another inmate with a lock in a sock, wreaking some vengeance on their head for some perceived disrespect that occurred that day. And if they awaken having to go to the bathroom, they wait until their homeys are up so their bathroom visit does not become a trap for them being raped or a beat down from rival gang members. They never know if just coming back from a chapel service, where they have spent a spirit lifting hour, will turn into a fight for their life with an inmate who is waiting for them to return to the unit and jumps them in an entry way.

I'm not telling you this for a sympathy play. They did the crime. They have to do the time. But those of you that minister in jails and prisons should remember the environment the inmates live in. The gospel you bring may be literal life and death. The verse I have given many of them wrestling with fear does bear out in their reality.

> I will lay me down in peace, and sleep, for Thou oh Lord makes me to dwell in safety." (Psalm 4:8)
>
> Whether I live I live to the Lord, whether I die, I die to the Lord, so whether I live or die, I am the Lords. (Romans 14:8)

That counsel may seem like offering them a sugar pill for fighting their monsters, but more times than not, it encourages these men and women to a literal faith in God to protect and deliver them while they endure incarceration and the real life-and-death issues all around them. So keep it real. Make the most of every conversation you have with an inmate. Because if they keep coming back to these dark places of human deprivation, there is a real possibility they just may meet the Master sooner rather than later.

CHAPTER 30

Mass Murderer

Boom! My house that was twenty miles away literally shook when the shock wave of the blast hit. The Murrah Federal building in Oklahoma City had just blown up. For days afterward, a shocked nation wondered. Who? What? When? Where? What do we do now?

According to the *Encyclopedia of Oklahoma History*, this man's actions impacted the nation greatly, "killing 168 people and injuring approximately 850." The governor's office reported that 30 children were orphaned, 219 children lost at least one parent, 462 people were left homeless, and 7,000 people lost their workplace. Not to mention the "estimated property damage to more than three hundred buildings in a forty-eight square block area" (OKhistory.org-Oklahoma Historical Society). All this by a couple of angry men who had concocted a plan to hit the nation that gave them birth with a concoction of fertilizer housed in a truck and parked in front of that federal building. America had been hit hard by an act of terrorism long before the Twin Towers.

In the days following, it was *not* business as usual. The perpetrator of the heinous crime was being housed initially at the federal prison in El Reno, just outside of Oklahoma City, where I worked as a chaplain. Problem: one of the correctional officers' wives had been on the fourth floor when the building was blown up. Other officers were helping with the rescue mission on their own time. Would they be able to maintain their professionalism when touched so closely with the crime of this man? It would not do for a person so close to the tragedy to decide to perpetrate personal vengeance on their charge. The majority of staff would be able to deal with the horror with honor and professionalism and did for over a week. However, the upper echelon was taking no chances. Over a period of several days and weeks, ranking officers from various prisons throughout the country were flown in to stand watch over the man.

It's no small thing to question the integrity of men and women trained to respond professionally in such situations, especially in the midst of the unfolding events. But higher-ups were taking no chances and decided not to allow local prison staff to stand watch on this inmate. But maybe that decision was best for them. There was no need to add to the impact the personal variables were having on the staff.

The perpetrator and his cohort were housed in a wing of the holdover far downrange and isolated from everyone but the select officers. I hadn't asked to see him. It wasn't time, and I was busy for days dealing with the staff that were dealing with the atrocity. They were coming back to work having been at the site searching through the rubble for survivors. My days were spent at the home of the officer who waited in vain with his two small children for his young wife whose body would not be found in the rubble for almost a week. His nightmare was not going to be over.

Then came the call for a chaplain to go to that wing. The mass murderer wanted to see a chaplain. Interesting. Well, okay. I went. The wing was empty except for the visiting ranking officer sitting in a chair not far from the cell. I signed in at the book designed to monitor the goings and comings of any staff in the area. After greeting the lieutenant, I made my way down to the cell. The food slot was open. The window slit in the door revealed a thin-faced, medium-sized military-type man with strawberry-blond hair styled in a crew cut. He was clad in an orange baggy jumpsuit and was standing by his metal bunk. He had the face of anyone you'd see on the street, and certainly the face of anyone you'd see on a military base. He had no horns, but his eyes were empty of anything but a steel resolve. He had accomplished his self-imposed mission. No regrets here.

I don't know why, but I reached inside the open food slot and extended my hand. He looked at my hand and then at me. He then grasped and shook my hand. I think my action startled him. I introduced myself as the chaplain and said I was there in response to his request. His need? He had been receiving bibles in the mail from Christians, total strangers, intent on saving his soul. He wanted to donate them to the chapel. My only question was "You sure you don't want to keep one?" "No, I'm sure." This homegrown terrorist had set his course. He had made up his mind. He was sure.

He handed them one by one through the food slot. The last one was a particularly nicely bound bible in fine leather.

"Thanks," I said dispassionately. "I'll make sure they are given to the men."

I didn't think about those words then, but now I think they were profound. *The men*. There were other men in this prison too. Real men. These men were incarcerated having acted out in their own way against society. The men who had looked themselves in the face and didn't like what they saw and were making changes while imprisoned; real men who were facing their failures and using their failures to move forward rather than allowing their disappointments to make them bitter; the men who were finding their true strength and the meaning to life in their relationship with Christ; the men who just might turn their life around and impact their society in a positive way. Real men understand their frailty and, from that realization, put their trust in God and find their true power. The men, whom Satan had intended for the dung heap, now were seeing life as something worth the living because of this Bible this mass murderer had handed so cavalierly through the food slot.

This mass murderer may have thought his action was justified by his puffed-up ideology that sanctioned his strike at a nation that had given him birth and, by his assessment, had betrayed his trust. But in acting on his bitterness, he became a poster child for the sayings "When you seek revenge, dig two graves-one for your enemy and one for yourself" and "Bitterness is like drinking poison and expecting the other person to die."

In McVey's case, his bitterness gave him permission to blow up a building with children, mothers and fathers, brothers and sisters, aunts and uncles, all just living their lives, for some warped sense of vengeance.

Years later, I participated with other chaplains and psychologist role-playing rioters prepping Special Ops Response Teams for possible physical conflict and civil unrest prior to the execution of this orator of distorted principle. It was thought there would be loud verbal protest outside the prison as the United States resumed the death penalty. Ordinarily, those against the death penalty will show up to protest. And there were some. Strangely, I remember no real media-covered protest being reported surrounding McVey's death. This reprobate, who had murdered innocent civilians for a perverted earthly cause, had no real supporters. It seemed his actions had silenced them too.

CHAPTER 31

Gangster Pride

I stood outside the hospital room and greeted the officers sitting outside at the door. They were *sitting on* the high-profile patient, an inside phrase for duty guarding someone at a local hospital. There was a middle room to pass through before actually entering his room. I stepped just inside and paused. It seemed surreal, me standing in the dark room looking through into the brighter room housing the most notorious gangster in America. His bed was framed by the door, and it was almost like looking at some painting. It was a small room on an upper floor, but his bed was by a huge window. He lay on the freshly starched white-sheeted bed with the light from the window streaming like a spotlight into the room. No color, just light, with no golds, reds, blues, or greens, just various hints of gray. Strangely, it symbolized to me what his life had become as he lay there, his still breathing body a symbol of his life of wrecking decay and death. He was no longer the swaggering, well-dressed powerful man he had been years ago in his prime. He had owned the streets. The man who had once ordered the deaths of many now had been silenced by the disease that had attacked his vocal chords. He lay in the stillness like a photo-capturing time, his head turned, staring out, lost in his thoughts.

Weeks earlier, he had arrogantly challenged the system housing him, blowing up at a chaplain from his own traditional religious persuasion. Why was he kept segregated from the main population? He had challenged arrogantly. His knew his only true power came from his influence and the validation he got from the minions and the masses sold out to his handouts and protection he gave them. Without them, he was only man. When told it was for his own safety, he clothed in his baggy orange jumpsuit, a far cry from the designer suits once worn, blurted viciously, "*My* protection? People need to be protected from *me*!" That chaplain never went back.

Now he was dying. In this moment of his true vulnerability, obviously an encounter set up by God, I entered the room. He turned his head slowly and looked at me. There was no arrogance today. I was meeting the real man. His eyes were sad, distant, still lost in his thoughts. He didn't want to come back inside the room, wanting to stay in the freedom of this mind, probably able to move freely and be surrounded and loved by his family. Yes, even the bad guys have people who love them. These things are the things that make for happiness. Too late, perhaps, he was realizing that.

I introduced myself as the duty chaplain. The presence of God was what I had to offer. I told him I was praying for him and his family and that I knew it must be hard on them, not being able to be around him while he was so sick. He nodded slightly and quietly thanked me. He returned to staring out the window as I turned to go. I don't remember saying a verbal prayer. Maybe I did, but I don't know.

I left, greeting once again the officers who were guarding the man. Even in his fragile state, he had enemies and friends that would have risked getting at their charge. The officer's stress was reduced by the presence of God too, and they momentarily were able to smile as I bantered with them on my way out.

I've thought of that scene often over the years. Did I miss an opportunity to once again present Christ to this man? All I know is I also keep hearing the echo of his arrogant words to the other chaplain, "My protection? People need to be protected from me!" ringing in my ears. These are not the words of a man who will have a deathbed conversion. I had prayed for direction when I entered the room. What I had said was all I was supposed to say. I can only imagine if on this earth he didn't get things right with God, that his arrogance and posturing will not deter judgment. I will always wonder. I think I know, but only in eternity are the results of a man's life tallied. But I do know some people just do not repent, not even on their deathbed.

CHAPTER 32

Out of the Gang and into the Fire

He'd been in the gang for years. He'd joined to survive. He'd risen through the ranks by becoming an enforcer. Hurting people was an extension of his own continual existence. But inside he was living a lie. He didn't want to hurt people. Every time he followed an order from the gang hierarchy, he felt like he was killing himself. He hated seeing the fear in the man's eyes when he knew gang justice was coming. He hated it with every blow he dealt. But he was good at it, mostly because he never did anything half way. Oddly, however, his conscience caused him to pummel himself more.

He wanted out, but once in a gang, there was no way out but his own encounter with gang justice. He'd seen what happened to men who tried to leave the gang. They knew too much and were a liability. So he kept marching to the sound of the gang's beat, lying, cheating, stealing, fighting, wounding, doing drugs, and having any woman he wanted. At least he had a place in this life. It was what he knew. It was his family. But his heart ached. There had to be more.

Then he was invited by his cellmate, by his own description "a religious kook," to attend a special service in the chapel. He went because there were going to be good-looking women in the choir. Some of his fellow gang members went too. They sat in the back row, snickering at the other inmates attending. What a joke. But the women were fine.

But while he joined in the ridiculing along with his compadres, inwardly, he was surprised. He was greeted by other inmates in a natural way, a genuine friendly fashion he'd not been used to. They knew the prison hierarchy, but it didn't matter to them he was in a gang and someone to be feared on the compound. The chapel, most of the time, was neutral ground. He observed a family atmosphere between the inmates attending. This was not the kind of family that brought a beating if you violated some rule. He was in a family too, but the gang family had conditions, and if they weren't met, prompt punishment was administered. The Christian guys accepted him as he was and in friendship, offering him inclusion on the common ground of faith. These men laughed and sang and had a good time, and it didn't include fear.

The music was great and opened up his heart to hear the preacher. The preacher didn't speak condemnation but truth. His words cut to his heart. He started listening. That night, he couldn't sleep as the words repeated over and over in his mind. This wasn't some pie-in-the-sky message. It had meat to it, and his soul reached out and took the hand Jesus was extending to him right there as he lay in his cell longing for more.

He didn't want to be one of those jailhouse religion converts who all of a sudden started to carry their Bible around and put their nose up in the air. He kept silent about his conversion and secretly began to read his cellmate's Bible when he wasn't around. Every time he did, he felt his heart grow calmer. Faith started to grow as he became acquainted with his new *gang* leader. Before long, he couldn't keep it to himself and told his cellmate.

His cellie was bold and honest with him. There was no such thing as a silent Christian, he learned. Well, okay, then. He'd faced death before for all the wrong reasons. At least now he'd face death for all the right ones.

He made an appointment with the prison gang leader. He told him about his conversion. He told him he wanted out, that he couldn't live this way anymore. He was told he'd have to petition the head of the whole gang, who was housed in another prison, for permission to withdraw. It seems like the only way a gang member could get out of that gang alive was on religious grounds. Even the bad guys have their code of ethics, warped though it may be. He followed the gang rules and solicited the leader's permission. There was one stipulation: live his faith. If he didn't, he'd get gang justice for lying just to get out. He agreed. He was out.

He was a true follower of Christ and sincere in his growth in the Lord. He was one of the most real Christians I'd ever discipled during my thirty years working in jails and prisons. Some might say he had more incentive to follow his faith, since if he didn't, it meant death. Maybe, but I don't think so. There was a real humility about this man. He put just as much energy into growing in the Lord as he did when he was enforcing the gang's rules. He didn't go around with his nose in the air being religious. He worked through genuine issues and got grounded in his faith. He was a smart guy and sensitive. I knew he'd always be tormented because of his past, like Peter. But like Peter, he made his peace because of the grace Christ gave him.

If you've worked in prisons long enough, you know chapels are not exempt from inmates whose bad behavior carries over to the area, threatening the peace of those who wish to use the space for its correct purpose. Chaplains are not exempt from being threatened or given a hard time by individuals or religious groups. I know I had my thorns in the flesh, which always made for tense moments in the chapel when they were there. But God works in mysterious ways. Not that any chaplain solicits an inmate's protection, but often I think there is a silent rule of respect from inmates watching the backs of fair corrections officers and chaplains. One thing is for sure, everyone with issues against rulings of chapel staff behaved themselves when one of these ex-gang enforcers turned Christian was in attendance at chapel services. I wonder why.

CHAPTER 33

Bluffing Crazy

He was a big guy—a good six-foot-two. I'm five-foot-six. He was a menacing man with short dreadlocks and a perpetual wild-eyed crazy look in his eyes. He had a tattooed teardrop on the left corner of one eye, a gang symbol meaning he had killed someone. He was also a member of a non-Christian group and one of their loose cannons. Even the hierarchy in his religious group and his gang always had their eye on him.

I guess it was in his nature, but he always seemed to have some beef he was bringing to me to fix, either personal or on behalf of his group. His reasoning and style of negotiating his request were pretty erratic, and most of the time, I just had to smile and send him on his way with his demands unmet. But, in some instances, I was able to intervene and fix some actual issues for him where he'd fallen through the cracks in the system of paperwork in the prison. I think that threw him off his disruption game in the chapel. Inmates didn't always like my decisions in the chapel, but one thing they did know, if they had a real need, I was the same with all of them, regardless of religion.

There were many times I was the only chaplain working in a chapel full of male inmates. I know I went through several angels, and many times my guardian angel had to call for backup. One such time involved this guy. Religious holy days sometimes involve a lot of preplanning because of issues that may run into conflicts with regular meal times. The inmates who wanted to participate in such a holy day had to make sure they signed up by the stated deadline. He missed it. Prior to his regular religious service where at least fifty of his cohorts were gathering for prayers, he stomped into my office—yes, stomped—making his case to participate formally with his group even though he'd missed the deadline. I held firm.

He stomped into his group service, where he concocted a story of discrimination and mistreatment. After their service was over, I was minding my own business in the outer foyer of the chapel waiting for the formal move where inmates could go back to their units. Out came this inmate and three of the group leaders, several of whom were gang leaders. They approached me, taking up his cause. Instead of asking to talk in the office, the disgruntled crazy guy began to make his case in front of the three, and then, to my dismay, all the remaining members, about thirty or forty, filed out into the foyer to wait for the move to the unit. By the nature of the location, I was immediately surrounded by a hoard of potentially angry inmates taking up the cause. Not good.

I had three choices: faint dead away, which was not an option, and, truthfully, I was feeling more like doing a David and Goliath rather than feeling fear; push my radio alarm, which would result in dozens of staff running to my aid and making this into a bigger deal, an option that frankly never came to my mind; or, three, pretend being surrounded by tattooed gang members championing a religious cause was all in a day's work and just take care of business and deal with their leaders with confidence.

I did the latter. I told them his error and how he'd lied to the group regarding his actions and then pointed out he was pulling the whole group into his cause, which could shut them down for any group activity. I told him he needed to be responsible for himself without pulling them into his bad behavior. I told them they were welcome to take this up with the lieutenant, but that unless they wanted to come to my office and talk this through in a civil manner, they could plan to do their religious holy days in the segregated housing unit. My bluff apparently worked. The leaders said they'd come and talk later about it and made the errant inmate stand down.

I remember pulling my radio during the foyer discussion and asking for the compound officer to step to the chapel. I also remember peripherally seeing a couple of the inmate leaders standing behind this guy as though keeping an eye on him. Regardless of their hostile disagreement with me, I concluded the inmates did not want to be responsible for this guy punching out a chaplain. There's no honor in that. Even inmates have a code. But the leaders had spoken, and he was bound to their rules. I do remember Crazy Guy looking at me with kind of a mocking grin that he'd been able to front me out in front of the hoard. But I also saw looks from his cohorts and gang leaders I interpreted as a grudging respect that I had stood up to Crazy Guy and them. I think I passed some kind of test.

Crazy Guy later lay in wait for an unfortunate fellow inmate and beat the pulp out of him and landed in segregation charged with assault and spent the religious event in segregation. God works in mysterious ways. There's no doubt in my mind this inmate would have had no problem assaulting me.

I look back at that and several other incidents like it. I take no credit for pulling off the bluff with this guy. God gives us the wisdom to think on our feet when we are in the middle of a fray, and He makes sure we have backup when we're doing His will. Master Control later told me they were watching on the cameras, just waiting for me to give a signal I needed help. I had forgotten about the cameras. I could tell I had gained their respect too. After all, the officers in the unit are often alone with several hundred inmates who frequently get angry at them.

I am often asked if I'm scared when I enter the prison each day. My response has always been that I have a healthy caution, but it's what I'm called to do, so I just do the job without really thinking what could happen. I think of the verse "Touch not mine anointed and do my prophets no harm." Maybe the inmates that day didn't hear that audibly. They were too busy seeing the angel standing behind me with the flaming sword, and that was enough for them.

CHAPTER 34

Dead Woman Walking

She was turning tricks at age eleven. She didn't have to hide it from her mother. It was her mother that had turned her out. It was a strange form of child abuse, and it had the same result most kids experience when a parent is the source of their pain. They try to please them. It's not the abuser's fault, they conclude, so it must be theirs. She brought in a lot of money. It paid the bills. It paid for the drugs. But she lost her childhood. By her early twenties, she had done it all and now had found a pseudo love with a local hit man.

Then it all came tumbling down. Her mother died. Emotional anger had taken root, unreconciled by her mother's irrational abuse. Her mother now became deified in her mind, the ugly betrayal of motherhood pushed into oblivion. When, in a fit of anger, a male friend rips up the last pictures of her mother, she concocts revenge against him. In the dead of night, she and her hit man boyfriend break into his apartment to steal his beloved motorcycle he keeps inside. The plans go wrong. They had miscalculated, thinking he was out for the night. He wasn't. A fight ensues. The hit man takes a climber's pickax found in the corner of the bedroom and plants it in the man, leaving the man dead on the floor. The girl enters the room to steal valuables. A sudden movement at the end of the bed under the covers startles her. Motorcycle Man's girlfriend had visited on the wrong night. The drugged-out avenging girl engages her in a fight while calling for her boyfriend. He enters and kills the girl with the pickax. He leaves the room, but Motorcycle Man's girlfriend begins to gurgle, the blood seeping into her mouth from her lungs. The young drugged-out prostitute takes the pickax and buries it again in her chest. The gurgling stops, so does the life of the young eleven-turned-twenty-something drugged-out victim of a worthless mother. She got the death penalty.

But it doesn't end yet. Throughout years of waiting for trial, the trial, the death sentence, and the wait for the execution date, her life, now free of drugs and men, she was able to see clearly. Some call it jailhouse religion, a bargaining chip for reprieve from the needle, but she served the Lord while on trial and while on death row. She saved two of her fellow dead women walking cohorts from ending their own lives: one who also would go on to the execution chamber but the other whose sentence was commuted to life. She testified to guards and did community service, making dolls for abused children. But she never asked for reprieve. Others were asking for her, even the judge that sentenced her.

Her take on her situation? She said she deserved the sentence of death. It was just. She'd take the reprieve if it came and be a witness for the rest of her life in prison if given the chance. But she'd leave all that up to God. But her answer came, and the governor refused to commute her sentence to life.

I didn't get involved in her last days. I didn't write letters to add to the pile going to the governor. I had played a part in her early discipleship, and I had visited her on death row. I, like her, figured that was all in God's hands.

She gave me one of her dolls when I saw her last on death row. It had a full smile on its face, just like Karla always did those days. And it wasn't fake. A day before the execution, I called the chaplain there and told him to tell her I'd see her in heaven. I have no doubt I will.

CHAPTER 35

Staring into Nothingness

Grown men dressed in khakis standing in line for a meal in the prison chow hall, looking blankly into the ground, lost in private thoughts, the only privacy owned now. They have food, shelter, clothing, but not privacy. They gave up the right to privacy when they did the crime. Only in their thoughts do they have a private place.

Watching him somehow evokes a fleeting moment of empathy, even though the responsibility for being here belongs to them. I don't feel sorry for them, really. There's no time for that. These men are in the heat of battle. The outward appearance is merely standing in line waiting to eat prison chow. But this line is different from standing in one of a buffet. There is no choosing what they will eat or the time they will eat or with whom they will dine.

If one suddenly looked up and noticed I was watching them, I would look away if only to preserve their dignity in one small way. They get watched a lot. Nothing is private except their thoughts. They are the truly lonely in a crowd.

His arms are crossed now. The back of the inmate ahead of him is inches away and could make a blank canvas for his thoughts. Yet he looks off to the side and to the ground. Maybe staring at the back of the other inmate would be misinterpreted by prison survival code, thus staring into the ground is safer and further disengages him from human contact even standing in line. Ground is neutral. It's hard to imagine him able to detach from all the loud talk of some of the other men in chow line. Those who use noise to distract themselves are also lost in thought in a way. They engage the technique of pretending it's just another day of time in prison. Not that laughter is unusual in prison. It's human nature to want to laugh, to experience some moment of normalcy as a human being. Men don't leave their humanness at the entrance of the prison. But laughter has never meant inner peace.

What is that one thinking? It could be as deep as imagining himself with his wife or kids, or as deep as wondering what he's doing here. Some of the men are surprised by prison. Some are businessmen caught up in a shady deal, perpetuated by rationalization and compromise. Others were on a downward slide because of drugs and were so zoned out that when the drugs wore off and they started thinking clearly, they found that whatever nightmare they are trying to escape using drugs had just changed to the face of prison. Out of the frying pan into the fire.

Of course, staring off into nothingness doesn't always translate into deep thought. Some of these men never do anything about dealing with what brought them to prison. The blank stare into oblivion, the zoning out, is a survival method, a lot like a depressed person sleeping all the time. They tune out the noise, the people, the thoughts are tepid, their next steps robotic. They are just doing time. Some have mastered doing time without dealing with what brought them here. It's not so deep. Some people just don't have an interest in changing their ways. Crime is an art, a challenge. In prison, they just perfect their art.

Stoked from his private oblivion, the young man moves toward the food service, where he can at least feed his body. I can only pray he will get hungry enough to want to feed his soul too.

So I watch him as the chow line starts to move. The Savior is, in an eternal way, watching him too.

CHAPTER 36

The Encounter

I was between programing at the prison and went to the officers' break room to get a cola. The day was sunny but not too humid. Inmates were walking around going to rec, coming from the chow line or back to their unit. Closed movement hadn't been announced. I had thought to go back to the chapel but couldn't force myself yet to enter its coldness. And if I went inside the grill—terminology for the entrance to the inmate side of the compound. I'd be besieged with needy inmates wanting this and that. I needed a moment to chill. So I got off to the corner of the grill, just outside the secure area, stood in the shade, leaned on the wall, and started sipping my cola. The movement of the inmates reminded me of a busy city street with coming and goings. The three sidewalks streaming from the three two-story units merged in the middle, and every now and then, familiar greetings, unusual handshakes, pats on the back, or even man hugs were exchanged. I tried to focus on individuals or small groups, but, soon, the steams of movement mesmerized me, and it again turned into a constant flow of imprisoned humanity, popping up every now and then for individuality, then deflating back into the human river.

Then an angry man emerged from the stream and headed in the direction of the lieutenant's office, which was right in front of where I was standing. My first inclination was to retreat into the shadow to be left alone, but that feeling only lasted a moment as the still small voice reminded of my purpose in being here at all. God sets us up for these encounters. He positions us, then sends the person in need our way. That's how I saw it and stood my ground.

The man stomped my way, brow creased with anger, mouth tight lipped, hiding clenched teeth. His eyes were cast down as were his shoulders, completing the picture of a man pressured to fury, a human bomb waiting to explode. Yet he was oblivious to me until he was a few feet away when he looked up. I saw the conflict in his face as he fought through the rage to assess who I was and how I was going to receive him. Was I another adversary that needed to be braced against, another set to assault his emotions in this place? So I smiled. Again, the conflict wrestled with his face as some of the tension in the brow relaxed, and a slight light in his eye glinted of hope. It was as quickly gone.

But I followed the smile with "Well, it looks like you're having a bad day." Risky. Using humor to attack pain always is. But it was as if a wand was waved across the tension in his face. His expression turned into a hint of a guarded relief.

He smiled quickly, then his brow furrowed as he said, "Yeah, that lieutenant is just picking on me. He stopped me for nothing and started harassing me, and I lost my cool, and he told me to go wait by his office until he came."

"Well, that couldn't have been fun especially in front of all the other men passing by," I said, with another attempt to reduce the intensity. "So, you been here long? I don't think I've ever seen you around before." Diversion. His face was again in conflict. Should he stay in the fight frame of mind or welcome a real conversation with someone who was treating him as more than a number? He chose conversation, and we engaged in talking about his family and the length of his sentence.

But, after a while, it was time to come back to the issue at hand. "Let me give you a tip," I advised. "When the LT comes, just listen and say, 'Yes, sir.' In this environment, there are reasons an LT will do a random dress down with an inmate in front of others. It's the nature of the beast. But you also don't know the purpose, and, unfortunately, arguing with an LT will only provoke the situation against you."

He listened, and I continued. "I also don't believe this encounter with me was accidental either. Do you have a faith you follow?" He spoke of familiarity with God, but I could tell by his terminology he had no real relationship. I spoke of a God where there are no coincidences and the oddity of my presence at this time and place and how I believed this event occurred so that in some way God could meet him in this place. "Satan meant evil to you, but God means this for good."

He listened. He did not respond verbally, but he relaxed. He smiled. His face was changed. Rage had been overcome, and in its place was the ability to breathe and see a bit clearer regarding his situation. Our encounter illuminated the awareness of the reality that God was even in this place. And that seemed to change his whole countenance and provide him hope. It's not the first time I've seen a literal physical change wash over a person as a person feels the touch of God and rage is replaced by peace.

The move was over. I looked up and saw the lieutenant coming across the compound. He saw me too. His stern no-nonsense look changed as he saw me talking to the inmate he was coming to berate for motives justified or not. I reminded the inmate of what I said about how to address the lieutenant. He smiled and said okay.

I greeted the lieutenant, who happened to be one of my favorites. I saw the lieutenant's demeanor relax as he looked at me, then past me to the now calm inmate. He was perplexed, I think. I think he sensed something had occurred here. I believe God's grace washed the anger out of him too.

As I walked away, I heard the lieutenant address the inmate civilly about his behavior, and I heard a few "Yes, sirs." The inmate was sent on his way toward the chow hall. Odd, these types of encounters. It's that brush with the intricate plan of God in people's lives. If we are listening, we can participate in the awesome eternal work God is doing at that moment in time. It comes out of nowhere, and if we are perceptive and willing, we just might be the vessel God uses to give someone peace.

CHAPTER 37

Pagan with an Attitude

He was a leader in the Odinist pagan religious group, a spin-off of the more benign Asatru religion. The Odinist slant is mostly found in prisons and are usually affiliated with White Aryan groups who reject all other races. But since Odinist had kept the religious components of Asatru, they were allowed to have meetings so long as the racist component was not practiced.

When I came to that facility, I assessed all the groups including present practices, and if there was a question, I sought outside representatives from their religion as well as the regional chaplain to validate the claims. After assessing this group, I halted the digging of a two-foot firepit and confiscated the two-foot wooden sword, all of which had been "homemade" by the inmates. Who would not know inmates can't have a sword or have firepits to jump, presenting certain hazards in a secure environment? Don't get me started on these easy-touch chaplains who would rather be liked by the inmates instead of making unpopular security decisions necessary for a correctional environment. But that's another story.

All that was really required by this group were some type of flame and symbolic ceremonies with lit candles. Services were rarely outside and not mandated. But this group insisted on accommodation, so a least restrictive balance was sought. That panned out to mean, from time to time, an outdoor ceremony would be allowed, but the chaplains would decide on how often. Outdoor accommodation for any pagan group was always subject to staff monitoring, which meant a chaplain had to be there, so outside ceremonies had to be scheduled when the main chapel was closed. And the only fire they could have would be a candle in a small metal pan, and certainly no sword, but a small cardboard cutout symbolizing a sword would be allowed. All fulfilled their ceremonial needs. Of course, that's a far cry from a blazing fire to jump and a sword to wave over their head, so that made them angrier.

When I showed the sword to the lieutenants and captain, their eyes widened with incredulity. They thankfully took my sword offering to use for a what-were-you-thinking and what-not-to-allow-inmates-to make show-and-tell for training staff. But I'm getting ahead of myself. Needless to say, the friction from this group was constant with chapel staff.

But that's just groundwork for the real story here. Their leader was always griping for more outdoor time and was angry about the items confiscated. He constantly stirred the cauldron of strife in the chapel. I continued to try to be fair about time and space but exhausted all my skills at trying to find the balance in a correctional environment.

Now, the following might make some people mad. Some might say you're a chaplain, not a cop. Sometimes, discipline needs to be harsh, but it is necessary to correct the behavior. God works in people's lives in ways we don't understand. Change is a journey from pain. Sometimes, a wound has to be lanced and cauterized before healing can take place. Hear me out on this.

I finally spoke to the captain about this inmate's constant disruption in the chapel. His fix-it method was epic. He called the inmate over to his office and had him patted down and then reamed him out. All the while, I had been told to stay in an office out of sight of the inmate. When the inmate started to lie about how he was being treated, the captain called me out of the office. The inmate paled. I've never seen a man physically drip drops of sweat after he saw me catching him in the lies. When the captain asked me if I wanted him to lock the inmate up, I said no. All I wanted was an attitude adjustment and to work out things with chapel staff constructively instead of keeping his group so upset all the time. The captain honored my request and sent him back to his unit.

Well, that seemed to do the trick. The constant outward tension died down. That inmate leader even sought me out in the middle of the compound in front of other inmates during a move and apologized for his behavior. But a forced apology was not an evidence of a heart that had been changed. I remained cautious and skeptical. But I committed to continuing to be fair with the group in spite of any future behavior.

Several weeks later, this man had a death in his family. It was tasked to me as the chaplain to inform him. I wasn't looking forward to it. I assumed I was going to be salt in his wound receiving such news from his perceived nemesis. But I called him over to the office and informed him of the death in his family and gave him phone calls to family.

Each person is different in how I minister to them. Usually, I open up with some type of grief counseling with the person but was not sure how with this man knowing our history of conflict and knowing where he stood religiously.

It was he who set the tone of the next few minutes. His ordinary puffed-up tense behavior softened, and his mask came off. He surprised me by thanking me for how I handled this. He then opened up about another death in his family. He had been in jail waiting to be sentenced when his child was killed in a wreck. The jail he'd been in allowed him to attend the graveside funeral. He shared that he had actually been a Christian at one time but became bitter when the preacher who did the graveside service made as part of his eulogy a pronouncement of guilt on this man, laying the ultimate responsibility for the child's death on how this man, her father, had been living his life. He said he became so angry that he vowed at that moment to never be a Christian again if guilt trips were how preachers and Christians dealt with a person's sorrow. He had been bitter ever since and had done every extreme thing, even to joining a pagan religion to strike at everything Christian.

Everything made sense now. He had been giving me trouble because he was angry with a preacher that, even though he had perhaps spoken the truth, had picked the wrong place and time for moralizing and had mangled the message of the gospel and its delivery with condemnation. That preacher hadn't told the man anything he didn't already know. He just ground salt in his wounds and picked at raw flesh. But, apparently, his interactions with me, including the shock and awe with the captain and the grace he received from me in not being locked in segregation, gave him a reality check of the grace of God. Weird how God works, huh? That abrupt intervention coupled with the grace he was receiving at the news of another death with no attached condemnation allowed God to pull the dagger of bitterness out of his heart and start his healing. Before he left, I was able to pray with him and told him he was welcome to come back if he just wanted to talk.

You never know what piece of another person's puzzle you are playing in their relationship with God. I prayed he would return to the Lord in full. Maybe he did.

CHAPTER 38

The Miracle of Our Faith

What would it be like to feel all your strength leave your body inch by inch? Each day becomes a new challenge as the things you used to do, like reaching for a glass of water, flipping on a light, or simply pulling the cover up for warmth, take all your concentration. Slowly, even the ability to move your mouth in tangible communication leaves. Inmates get such sicknesses too, and the worse off are sent to corrections medical centers best able to care for end-of-life issues. But it never ceases to amaze me when I see a Christian inmate with such a disease. Their very life becomes aglow and centered on Christ. They are up for hours before Chapel to be ready for church. They are often found waiting in their wheelchair by elevators and in hallways waiting on the "ride" to Chapel, a healthy inmate who pushes them to Chapel. Testimony time finds the incarcerated Body of Christ intently listening to understand the words, struggling from the mouth of these individuals. But the struggle is not for a show of strength but for praise to the Lord, who they see just over the horizon.

Wheeled purposefully into the chaplain office, on their way from Chapel, these inmates, who should need encouraging, lift the spirits of the chaplain by straining the words through their pain, "I ... am ... praying ... for ... you ..., Chaplain." And with a twinkle in their eyes and a knowing glow on their face, they are whisked away to their room to lie in bed for hours in communion with God. You can see the radiance coming from the face and light in the eyes, conveying a peace no person could explain in the light of the physical infirmity. Truly, this is the miracle our faith.

No matter your beliefs and experience with jail and prison ministry, there's no doubt God can bring peace and release to the hearts of the incarcerated. Staff and inmates bless us as we seek to bless them. It's something we can't comprehend but often experience in this ministry of faith. And guess what, when we get to heaven, those who have engaged in jail and prison ministry will be inundated with the hugs and thanks from all who were blessed by their willingness to enter the dark pits that are our jails and prisons with the light of the gospel of peace. No doubt, the Lord Himself will say, "Well done, good and faithful servant."

EPILOGUE

A FINAL WORD

THE POLITICS OF CHAPLAINCY

You might think it's strange to have an epilogue of this nature ending the book. It's not off topic at all. This has to be said to maintain the integrity, if not even the existence, of professional chaplaincy and volunteers in ministry in jails and prisons. Nothing could be more important than the leadership God has placed in secular places.

Chuck Swindoll, renowned pastor and teacher, made this comment in the note section of his study Bible.

> One person in a strategic spot who is walking with God can do a world of good. They can influence others. They can bring reproof. They can model Godly character. They can simply be involved in the stream of life ... Our tendency is to underestimate the value of our relationships with people outside the family of God. But if we are walking with God, we are already in a strategic position. Thank God if you are in the stream of the unsaved. (The Swindoll Study

Bible, Tyndall House Publishing NLT, pg1099 Zephaniah comment)

It's imperative that those in ministry in secular situations never lose sight of their mission and handle it with integrity without allowing the interference of secularist misinterpreting the constitution. The attack on chaplains and as a consequence religious volunteers is something the church must pay attention to. No sitting on the sidelines. The secularist would like nothing more than to keep the church behind its own walls and out of the marketplace. Several times in my years of chaplaincy, I ran into those who would abolish chaplaincy and replace them with sterile religious program coordinators all in the name of budget and separation of church and state. Nowhere in the scripture or our Constitution does it ever promote the ghost law of the so-called separation of church and state.

People cannot be separated from their search for God. Jails and prisons are compelled by the First Amendment to respond to the religious needs of inmates. That's why chaplains are recruited for full-time staff positions in many institutions. What you run into in chaplaincy, whether it be jail or prison or even industrial and military, is the secular system trying to somehow dictate how religion functions in those systems. That automatically engages that natural tension of religion and the secular. The secular seeks boundaries on religious expression so as not to offend, but religion is like a mist that transcends boundaries. The secular by its nature jealously demands control and the ability to audit religious expression, while the religious only recognize God as their ultimate authority and see government as an extension of the will of the people meant only to protect those rights. Why do you think every dictatorship takes and remains in power by abolishing or limiting religious expression? Religious faith promotes individual thought and has ultimate allegiance only to God. That threatens humanist and their power to influence society. Make no mistake, the wolves are always prowling at the door.

At present, in jails and prisons, secularists run into problems trying to water down religious expression. First Amendment rights for religious expression for inmates or staff doesn't stop when prison doors slam behind them. Thank God for our Constitution. They cannot ban religious expression outright in the name of security. Because of the nature of the institutional mission, government is forced to find ways to set boundaries only if that expression conflicts with the secure running of the institution.

Before the water gets too muddy on this subject, let me break it down as it pertains to chaplaincy in correctional institutions. What are the "political" tensions affecting chaplains serving in secular places? Two things: chaplains have to always resist the temptation to seek titles and status that can blur the boundaries in ministry; and, two, the ever-present intrusion of secularist bent on inserting pluralism in hiring practices to control religious expression that threatens their power.

Let me delve into the first tension: chaplain's face, the trap of losing your chaplain identity and seeking rank and status to dine at the king's table, so to speak. While a chaplain is wise to be well versed in the ins and outs of the correctional part of law enforcement, taking on roles in that system apart from their role as "sky pilot" is a tightrope act and, when failed, distorts the message to those they are called to serve.

When I was first hired in the Federal Bureau of Prisons, a regional administrator told me that my credentials impressed them. My bachelor of arts degree was in criminology as my original intention was to become a police officer. I chose to get my master's in education at the seminary and used that knowledge throughout my chaplaincy career developing seminars on corrections issues that would benefit corrections officers that in turn would benefit their care of inmates. I taught on issues of post-traumatic stress affecting officers involved in critical incidents on the job, loss of staff to inmate violence or being attacked, the ever-present uncertainty the administration would back them up in everyday decision-making, the ugly things staff see every day after inmate-on-inmate violence, law enforcement and suicide, grief and marriage counseling, critical incident and hostage training, inmate/staff conflict resolution, and teaching staff on the games inmates use to bait staff.

I took every required training staff had to take even to self-defense, weapons, and chase car and escort training. I stood with staff on cold mornings around burning barrels during annual training to keep warm waiting for my turn at weapons qualification, not so much to gain the skill but to know what the staff had to go through. If they had to do it, I did it too whether it was required of my role or not. My motive was to be a better chaplain to inmate and staff. I didn't want my ministry to be book learning or be motivated by some hidden desire to be "one of the boys" on a climb up the professional ladder. If a chaplain is doing it right and fulfilling their role, they are accepted and trusted and respected, but the goal should never to be *one of the boys.*

All those self-educating efforts didn't go unseen. Indeed, several times, I was encouraged by wardens to cross over and get on track to becoming a warden. I thought about it. I told myself, as a warden, I could help the whole system become better because I'd be functioning from a decision-making base in the institution. But crossing over also meant not making waves when waves were called for and playing politics to climb that ladder. That was a problem for me. It boiled down for me to the question of, What was my mission? What had God called *me* to do in this season of life? For a while, I left the door open. After all, God's people are not one note, having many talents. The early followers were tax collectors, fishermen, tentmakers, and doctors and plied other trades. Being called to ministry doesn't mean you set aside your other skills. He uses all of you. But there is a fine line between using your talents that aren't specifically seen as religious and separating yourself from your role as a chaplain.

So, in practice, I had no issue during disturbance lockdowns, helping push food carts to units and helping officers feed units and helping with official counts, doing rounds to take the wind out of inmate tension. Most often, even during disturbances and lockdowns and twelve-hour shifts, I functioned in a pastoral role, walking the units, tending to the concerns of the inmates, and joking around with staff, all of which could help reduce the institutional tension both for inmate and staff. Only in rare situations such as those riots did a warden ask me to fill a role other than my official title, such as keeping a running log in the command center until more staff arrived to fill that role. I had no issue with filling the gap in those ways because it was still in my role as a chaplain, and I was helping.

Neither did I have issue when doing my unit rounds to segregation inmates to be used in fulfilling random request for my help that some may have seen as outside my scope. For instance, two officers had to move an inmate who was required to have three staff to move him. I was there. They requested I help, or they'd have a long wait for more staff at a shift change, making them go into overtime waiting for them. Helping their immediate problem to me was ministry to them and building trust. It told me they knew I'd have their back should anything go down untoward. So, there I was holding the baton, walking behind two staff and a martin-chained and shackled inmate who was doing life, guilty of having killed a staff member and another inmate. Ministry takes many forms and often is a judgment call in the moment.

Where I drew the line was when the secular system sought to augment me to fill post in units when the system was failing in reaching staffing levels. They used the mantra that we are all corrections officers first. I was being ordered to staff a unit out of my role as a chaplain in a *routine* rotation not associated with lockdown situations. That would cause me to have to shut down chapel programs, neutralize my title of chaplain as well, and, by participation, relegate religious programming and chaplaincy to nonessential. To me, if I danced back and forth in the role from chaplain to corrections officer in the unit officially, staff and inmate would be confused and effectively neutralize the role of chaplain. I respectfully said no.

Yes, I received pushback from the higher-ups. They used as precedence against me other chaplains who had, during nonemergency situations, willingly sought out overtime for extra pay and filled nonchaplaincy posts. Those chaplains had unwittingly distorted the lines, and it had run downhill, affecting the whole perception of chaplaincy. But I held firm through official memos, stating my case all the way to the regional director. They ultimately were unwilling to push the issue with me, though one regional director I respected and had worked with when he was a warden actually tried to shame me with the implication I was shirking my duty. I laid out my case, listing historically and spiritually all I had and was willing to do, and they finally left me alone.

God's chaplaincy leadership will have struggles walking the fine line in the secular world of jails and prisons. If they take their mission seriously, they will, by their very presence, cause tension in that system. They have to be willing to deal with that tension and be willing not to be popular with the higher-ups that have influence over promotions or even be willing to appropriately challenge decisions that skirt into the realm of neglect or even wrongdoing by the system. That means they have to find the balance between following the structure needed by a semimilitary organization and staying true to the voice of the prophet standing in the gap, calling attention to cracks in that system that are affecting staff and inmate.

The second tension is the attempt at censorship of chaplains whose religious beliefs conflict with acceptance of popular social issues affecting the country. It's not only our military chaplains that come under attack. Chaplains in corrections also find themselves critically scrutinized. Chaplains have to be willing to speak truth to power whether it's on behalf of inmate or staff. They must be true to scripture while balancing the responsibility to the duty for which they are hired.

For instance, as a minor example, I once was placed on the institutional Christmas committee in charge of Christmas package distribution to inmates. I walked into the first meeting and casually asked if this was the Christmas meeting. A snarky associate warden immediately corrected me, saying, "It's a holiday committee." I replied, if he wanted to call it a holiday committee, fine. But my tradition calls it Christmas, and so I would continue to do so. That didn't go over well. It wasn't that I was disrespecting him. While that may seem a small matter some may say should have been ignored, it's that reasoning that starts erosion. It was the fact he was creating a policy regarding my traditions, not to mention the traditions of 90 percent of the inmates that was not even official policy coming down from higher-up. While I respected his role, I did not respect his attempt to censor my expression of the season. He was simply deciding he'd be politically correct and wield his personal power into an area in which he had no authority. He had it in for me after that.

The secular routinely pushes pluralism. The idea all religions are on an equal plain directly opposes the reality most that most religions feel they are exclusive, believing theirs is the only one way to God. Chaplains routinely bump into struggles with the secular as it attempts to control religious expression in the name of pluralism so as not to offend anyone. They become the thought police in a backdoor attempt to curb religious correction on moral issues some in society have embraced.

Chaplaincy job qualifications sometimes bleed over into censorship in the requirements for the hiring and credentialing of chaplains. Litmus tests for pluralistic views are subtle. They may try to credential out more conservative evangelical denominations by placing into job descriptions requirements not in tune with those denominations. That stonewalling of candidates might have gone unchecked had the candidates not made the case that government had no right to decide what a denomination required for their clergy. Those efforts have been thwarted so far, and those backdoor efforts forced to alter those requirements by adding exceptions for those applying for jobs from those denominations that don't fit the mold the government tried to create. God's people are a formidable force when living their mission outside the walls of the church. It is not a malicious rebellion against authority. They only seek to practice their faith without the government setting standards that lead to censorship of sincerely held beliefs.

We have great biblical models for working inside the secular. Esther, Daniel, Abraham, Moses, Joseph, Nehemiah, and other examples in scripture all at one time had the ear of kings during conflicts in their spiritual role in the secular government because they carried out their duties humbly but without compromise.

Government shouldn't presume to tell any clergy how to preach a sermon or compromise the teachings of their faith on any subject. Censorship should always be challenged. The point is chaplains are hired knowing they come from various belief backgrounds. And unless that religion fully applied poses a security issue within the prison, and some do, the least restrictive boundaries for practice and a hands-off policy should be the name of the game.

Integrity to the mission of chaplaincy produces influence. A multitasking and savvy person who is able to have insights into the mission field in which they function has a huge amount of influence on those in secular power. They won't always like what you have to say, but they will listen and may, down the line, correct something you pointed out.

The voice of God's people in taking the gospel mission to the world is hard under attack by those who would take God out of the jails and prisons, much less as a voice in the daily operations of our country. We do not have to blend into the secular and lose our identity to do that. We should do that unashamed by who we are and who we represent. It's past time for the Body of Christ to realize that there is no place in our country where we should not be involved. We are to take the gospel everywhere without compromise. If we don't do so boldly, a government out of its lane will do away with religious freedoms and replace it with counterfeit answers to society's problems. If chaplaincy ministry to jails and prisons is watered down by pluralism or, for that matter, replaced with secular program coordinators, I fear God's people will have been culpable in its demise if not in practice by complacency in what ground we cede to humanism.

Printed in the United States
by Baker & Taylor Publisher Services